بســـم الله الـرحمـــن الـرحيـــم

IRAN

A Chronological History

IRAN

A Chronological History

Saeed Alizadeh
Alireza Pahlavani
Ali Sadrnia

IRAN: A Chronological History
Authors: Saeed Alizadeh, Alireza Pahlavani, Ali Sadrnia
http://www.iran-history.com/
e-mail: info@iran-history.com
Phone: (+98 21) 205 8833

Designed and Published **2002** by the authors
ISBN 946-06-1413-0
First Edition, 3000 copies
Printed in Iran

فهرست نویسی پیش از انتشار

علیزاده، سعید، ۱۳۳۷- Alizadeh, Saeed
(ایران: ا کرنولاجیکال هیستری) Iran: a chronological history
Saeed Alizadeh, Alireza Pahlavani, Ali Sadrnia
۲۷۲ ص. ISBN 946-06-1413-0
فهرستنویسی بر اساس اطلاعات فیپا .
واژه نامه .
نمایه .
۱ . ایران -- تاریخ -- گاهشماری ۲ . ایران -- تاریخ نویسی.
الف. پهلوانی، علیرضا، ۱۳۵۲ - Pahlavani, Alireza
ب. صدرنیا، علی، ۱۳۴۰ - Sadrnia, Ali
ج.عنوان: Iran: a chronological history
۹الف۸ع / DSR۷۶ ۹۵۵/۰۰۷۲
۱۳۸۱ کتابخانه ملی ایران ۱۳۱۸۴-۸۱م

To our families
and friends

Acknowledgements

We, the authors of this book, are forever indebted to all those honorable scholars who have contributed to a fair and authentic introduction of Iran. Our heartfelt thanks are also extended to all those who gave us of their time, energy and resources. It is impossible to include here a complete list of credits, but the following friends and colleagues deserve special mention. We would like to express our sincere gratitude to Mrs Soudabeh Hassani and Mr Ebrahim Pour Faraj, the directors of Pasargad Tours, for their support and encouragement. Our special thanks are extended to Mrs Hedieh Azad, Mrs Mandana Vasigh and Mr Mohammad Reza Jafari for their advice and assistance. We like to express our great appreciation to our gifted editor, Mr Jamal Seyed Salehi. We are deeply grateful to Prof. Holly Pittman and Mr James Truman for commenting on the final version of this book. We must also thank Mr Ahmad Azad, Mr Ehsan Azish, Mrs Shima Sadra and Mr Mohsen Rami for their expertise and cooperation.

We would like to emphasize that the responsibility for any inaccuracy in this book lies with the authors, and no one else should be made responsible for any error or ambiguous phrasing. Furthermore, we'll be pleased to rectify any errors pointed out to us by our readers, to whom we shall always remain most grateful.

Preface

Iran, long known to the world as Persia, has been a constant source of fascination to the outsider for over two and a half millennia. This is not without good reason. Few countries in the world have been known to embrace as many civilizations and peoples as Iran, a fact that has earned the country the title "melting pot of civilizations".
With the vast heritage entrusted to us comes the responsibility of finding ways of guarding these cultural values, and identifying optimal ways of presenting them. As Iranian national guides, we felt a vacuum in the way our heritage is conveyed, especially to non-Iranians, who, if interested beyond the normal range of literature, are faced with voluminous and detailed accounts about the country. We set about the task of compiling this book with our professional experience leading the way: the sites we explain, the questions we are asked, and the enthusiasm we are shown.
In the execution of the project, we chose to incorporate all such factors and elements that have, in one way or other, contributed to the molding of modern day Persian civilization and culture. All the main entries are in black, and where necessary, complementary remarks printed in gray furnish additional information, which can be referred to for more detailed explanation. Hence, the format facilitates for the reader the selection of data according to its importance. Besides nearly all the major historical events, the entries also include the greatest achievements of the more prominent monarchs, religious figures, philosophers, politicians, poets, scientists, and historians, as well as significant historical monuments, and architectural innovations of artists who inhabited this land. In addition a glossary presents definitions and a guide to official titles, and four appendices present selected archaeological sites, a brief summary of prehistoric civilizations, a dynastic chronology, and a list of major figures of the Islamic faith.

Finally, we provide a comprehensive index of proper names and events listed according to date.
We aim at accuracy, understandability and ease of reference. However, we don't by any means consider the effort as infallible or complete; it is rather a starting point from which we can, with the feedback of our readers and colleagues, proceed to compile a collection that would satisfy the needs of all those whose interests cross paths with our own.
We are proud of "IRAN: A Chronological History", and dedicate it to all those who have a passion for this country.

Saeed Alizadeh, Alireza Pahlavani, Ali Sadrnia
Tehran – Autumn 2002

Contents

Achaemenian Period

550 – 330

The first great development of ancient Iran took place under the Achaemenid dynasty during the Persian Empire. The dynasty was named after Achaemenes, ruler of Anshan in the 7th century BC, but the real founder of the dynasty was Cyrus the Great, creator of the Persian Empire. At the zenith of their power the Achaemenids ruled an empire extending from the Indus River in the east to Libya and Thrace in the west and from the Persian Gulf in the south to the Caucasus and the Jaxartes River (modern Syr Darya) in the north. They provided Persia with superb administration, a comprehensive code of laws, reliable currency, and efficient postal service. Achaemenians were tolerant toward other religions, and under their rule, art and architecture flourished.

590 **Cyrus II was born.**
Cyrus II's father was Cambyses I, son of Cyrus I, King of the Persians, and his mother was Mandane, daughter of the Median king.

____ **Zoroastrianism was taking root in Persia at this time.**

____ **Some Persian tribes were settled and some were moving from nomadism to settled agriculture.**

586 The forces of the Babylonian Empire conquered Jerusalem. Babylonians destroyed their Temple and carried off a portion of the Jewish population into exile. The captives consisted mainly of educated and upper class people, and the royal family.

584 **Astyages became king of Media.**

563 Buddha was born in India.

561 Croesus became king of Lydia.

560 Croesus subdued Greek cities in Asia Minor.

559 **Cyrus II inherited his father's position as king of the Persians.**
Persian territory was within the Median Confederation up to this point.

555 Nabonidus became king of Babylonia.

551 Confucius was born in China.

550 **Having defeated the assault of Astyages at Pasargadae, Cyrus II deposed Astyages, united the Persians and Medes, and founded the first Persian Empire.**
Cyrus II, also known as Cyrus the Great, was an outstanding leader and skillful strategist. Cyrus was faced with two political objectives: He aimed at occupying the Mediterranean coast, and securing the defense of his eastern frontier. The Mediterranean coast and its seaports were terminals of the great trade routes crossing Persia. Nomadic tribes in the east were a potential threat to Persia's safety.

____ Sparta became supreme in the Peloponnesus, Greece.

____ **Cyrus II made an offer to Cilicia and Lydia, in southern and western Anatolia, to accept Persian sovereignty.**

At the Lydian capital of Sardis, the Lydian king, Croesus, sensed an impending threat from Persia.

549 **Darius, the future king of kings, was born.**

547 **Croesus mobilized his famous cavalry to attack Persia.**

546 **Cyrus II assembled his troops in Assyria, crossed the Tigris, marched towards Cappadocia, entered the seemingly impregnable Sardis, and defeated Croesus.**

Lydia was aided by Egypt, Babylonia and Sparta in the battle against Cyrus

Cyrus admired the beauty and grandeur of Lydia's architecture.

546 **Cyrus II established his capital city at Pasargadae.**

____ **Cyrus II once more took up wars of defense and conquest.**

____ **Asiatic Greek cities were conquered by Persia.**

540 **Cyrus II began his assault on Babylonia.**

539 **Cyrus II conquered Babylonia without any major clash of arms.**

Cyrus was about to play the part of intermediary between the western and eastern civilizations.

____ **Cyrus II liberated Babylonia from the oppressive rule of Nabonidus.**

____ **Nabonidus was taken prisoner, but Cyrus II treated him with clemency.**

In his conquests Cyrus adhered to the mandate of justice. He believed that God had entrusted him with the task of uniting the people in one kingdom of justice and peace. Cyrus had the wisdom to leave unchanged the institutions of each kingdom he annexed to the Persian Crown. He seized the hands of the statue of the city god Marduk as a signal of his willingness to rule as a Babylonian and not as a foreign conqueror. Cyrus presented himself to the Babylonian people as the legitimate successor to the Crown. Control of Babylonia meant overlordship of its dependencies, particularly Syria, towards which he pursued a benevolent policy.

____ The Phoenician rulers submitted to Cyrus II.

They offered their ships to Cyrus for military use against the Greeks.

538 Cyrus II issued a decree allowing the Jews to return home.

____ Cyrus II was acknowledged as a Liberator and a Messiah.

____ Nabonidus, the last king of the Babylonian Empire, died in captivity.

537 Cyrus II returned Jerusalem to the liberated Jews.

More than 40,000 Jews left Babylonia and returned to the Promised Land, but not all the Jews decided to go home. The adaptable Jewish people had established themselves in Mesopotamia, settling there and engaging in business and even politics. While remaining devout Jews, many of them decided to carry on their lives in their new home. Some of them even rose to high positions of service in the Persian imperial court.

This was the first significant contact made between the Jewish and Persian cultures.

For a decade the efficiently administrated empire generally lived in peace.

In a mere one generation Cyrus built an empire that stretched from Africa to China.

____ Cyrus II planned to conquer Egypt from Babylonia.

____ Cyrus II was forced to resume military operations against the nomads on the eastern borders of the empire.

____ Cyrus II left his son, Cambyses II, in charge of the military preparations for the Egyptian campaign.

534 Buddha propagated his teachings.

530 Cyrus II led his army across northeast where it engaged the Massagetaes.

The Massagetaes were a nomadic and hostile branch of the Scythians.

____ Cyrus II was killed in his battle against the Massagetaes.

____ **His body was brought to Pasargadae and laid to rest.**
Cyrus the Great was 'father' to Persians and magnanimous towards a defeated enemy, whom he endeavored to convert into a friend.

____ **Cambyses II, who was unlike his father in temperament and attitude, succeeded Cyrus II.**

____ **Cambyses II felt it necessary to murder his brother, Bardiya.**
His intention was to protect his rear while leading the Egyptian campaign.

525 **Cambyses II conquered Egypt and defeated pharaoh Psamtik III of the 26th dynasty.**
The rapidity with which Cambyses II initiated this successful campaign suggests that preparations for such an attack were well advanced under Cyrus. The sole achievement of Cambyses was in fact the conquest of Egypt.

522 **News reached Cambyses II of a revolt in Persia led by an imposter claiming to be Bardiya.**
The usurper was in fact a magus named Gaumata.

522 **On his way back from Egypt, Cambyses II quelled all challenge to his rule.**

522 **Darius raced homeward with his troops in order to crush the rebellion.**
Darius was a leading army general and one of the princes of the Achaemenian family.

522 **Darius in alliance with six satraps defeated and killed Gaumata.**

522 **Darius married both Cyrus II's daughter, Atossa, and the widow of Cambyses II.**

522 **Eight years after the death of Cyrus II, Darius was proclaimed the legitimate king, and ascended the Achaemenian throne.**
Darius was in the mold of Cyrus, a powerful personality and a dynamic ruler. During the first two years of his reign, he fought nineteen battles and suppressed all rebellions. He

recorded his victory in a gigantic bas-relief cut on a high cliff at Bisotun, in western Persia.

519 Xerxes, Darius' eldest son by Queen Atossa, was born.

518 Darius began the construction of the ceremonial capital of Persepolis.

517 Darius victoriously led his army into India.

516 Expansion in the west began when Darius moved against the Hellespont, now Dardanelles in northwestern Turkey.

This was the first step toward an incursion against the Scythians along the western and northern shores of the Black Sea.

515 The new temple was dedicated at Jerusalem after the return of Jews from the Babylonian captivity.

512 Darius drove the Persian army as far as the lower Danube.

____ Darius successfully led the campaign against the Scythians.

____ The empire that Cyrus the Great built and Darius defended and expanded was celebrated at Persepolis.

Persepolis was an elevated stage on which Achaemenians displayed the glories of Persia. On vernal equinox the Immortals, numbering 10,000, stood in attendance as the subject nations of the empire bearing gifts and tribute paraded past the Achaemenian throne.

The subject nations were the Medes, Susians, Armenians, Egyptians, Babylonians, Parthians, Cappadocians, Sagartians, Lydians, Gandarians, Scythians, Aryans, Arachosians, Cilicians, Drangianians, Indians, Ionians, Bactrians, Sogdians, Skudrians, Arabians, Libyans, and Ethiopians.

500 Monarchy ended in Rome and the Republic was founded.

499 The Ionian Greek cities on the west coast of Asia Minor revolted against Persian rule.

The Persians were apparently taken by surprise, and at first the rebellion succeeded.

498 The Ionians received limited assistance from the Athenians and felt strong enough to take the offensive.

Darius negotiated with one hand; with the other, he assembled a counter attack.

496 **The first Persian military onslaught against the Ionians proved only partially successful.**

The Ionians enjoyed another short-lived period of peace.

494 **A renewed Persian offensive proved successful.**

The Greek fleet was badly defeated off Miletus, western Anatolia. The Persian army began a systematic reduction of the rebellious cities.

492 **Mardonius, a son-in-law of Darius, was made special commissioner to Ionia.**

Having crushed the local tyrants, Mardonius recovered Persian Thrace and Macedon, and permitted a form of democratic government in many cities.

490 **Darius was defeated by the Greeks, under Miltiades, at the battle of Marathon.**

Having realized that the Greek problem would require a more concerted and massive effort, Darius began preparations for an offensive against Greece on a grand, coordinated scale.

486 **Darius the Great died at 63.**

Darius was the first monarch to understand that an imperial state could only exist if it evolved a coherent technological policy to keep the empire closely knit. Darius united and reshaped the nation, organized a highly efficient army and an administrative system, conquered and governed territories through satrapies held to Persia by means of an unmatched communication network of roads, of which the royal road stretching 2500 km (1500 miles) from Pasargadae to Sardis was the most important. He also undertook the construction of the precursor to the Suez Canal.

During the reign of Darius, the first steps were taken towards organizing a national economy. The introduction of a merchant navy, a banking system, coinage, a uniform weight and measures standard, as well as devising a perfectly balanced system of tax collection, were instrumental for more rapid internal trade development than foreign commerce.

A highly exceptional feature of the administration of Darius was its judicial system where royal judges interpreted national laws, judged cases, and were appealed to in all disputes throughout the empire.

A particular philosophical trait that Darius the Great evolved for the Persians was the spirit of nationalism.

486 **Xerxes, another outstanding ruler, became king of Persia.**

Xerxes continued to oversee the cross-fertilization of Persian culture encouraged by his fathers.

____ **Xerxes put the skills and talents of local and foreign architects and artisans to work at Persepolis.**

By this time Zoroastrianism that had gained influence since the reign of Cyrus II had systematized the empire's administration as a result of which a distinctive Persian culture had established itself.

____ **Xerxes married Esther.**

At the time of Esther, many Zoroastrians became Jews and most probably brought with them influences from their former religion.

____ The first Roman Land Reform was sanctioned by Spurious Cassius.

____ **Darius' death together with a serious revolt in Egypt, interrupted the plans against Greece.**

485 **Xerxes suppressed the revolt in Egypt in a single campaign.**

483 Buddha died at the age of 80.

482 **Plans for the invasion of Greece, begun under Darius, were still further delayed by a major revolt in Babylonia.**

____ **The revolt in Babylonia was crushed.**

481 **Xerxes marched out of Susa while in command of the biggest war machine ever mobilized in Asia to engage the Greeks.**

He spent the winter in Sardis and led a combined land-sea invasion of Greece.

480 **Northern Greece fell to the Persians.**

Persian forces marched on Athens, and burned the Acropolis.

____ **The Persian fleet lost the Battle of Salamis.**

The invasion lost its momentum, and Xerxes returned home, leaving Mardonius in charge of further operations.

479 **The real end of the invasion came with the Battle of Plataea, the fall of Thebes, which was a stronghold of pro-Persian forces, and the Persian naval loss at Mycale.**

479 Confucius, Chinese philosopher, died.

477 **Confederacy of Delos was founded by Athens for defense against Persia.**

465 **Battle of Eurymedon, in which Persians were defeated by Greeks under Cimon, was fought.**

465 **Xerxes was murdered by a palace conspirator.**

Achaemenian Persia began to decline. The occasional flashes of vigor and intelligence displayed by some of Xerxes' successors were too infrequent to prevent eventual collapse of the empire.

____ **Artaxerxes became king of Persia.**

____ **During the reign of Artaxerxes cultural relations with Greece extended.**

462 Sophocles and Euripides flourished in Athens.

____ Greek historians and scientists traveled in Egypt, Babylonia and Persia, and acquired further knowledge of the history, religion and sciences of the east.

____ Herodotus, born a Persian subject, wrote his history.

458 Ezra returned with many Jews from Babylonia to Jerusalem.

454 Athenian expedition to Egypt failed after initial success.

453 Treasury of Confederacy of Delos was removed to Athens and Athenian Empire reached its peak.

447 After the Greek victories over the Persians, construction of the Parthenon, an excellent example of Doric architecture, was commenced by Pericles.

445 Nehemiah began rebuilding walls of Jerusalem.

431 Peloponnesian War broke out between Athens and Sparta. This war lasted, with some occasional pauses, for about 37 years. Initially, the Persians lured Athens against Sparta which resulted in the treaty of Callias.

431 Herodotus, the Greek historian, died.

424 Artaxerxes died, and Xerxes II became king of Persia.

423 Xerxes II died, and Darius II became king of Persia.

422 Athenians were defeated by Spartans in the Battle of Amphipolis.

421 Peace of Nicias was maintained between Athens and Sparta.

418 Athenians were defeated by Spartans in the Battle of Mantinea.

413 After the disastrous Athenian campaign against Sicily, the Persians intervened on Sparta's side.

412 Persia recovered complete freedom in western Asia Minor. This was in return for consenting to pay seamen to steer the Peloponnesian fleet.

406 Euripides and Sophocles died.

405 Egypt revolted and Persia failed to maintain its sovereignty over it.

From this point on Egypt remained an independent state.

404 Persian gold and Spartan soldiers facilitated Athens' fall. Peloponnesian War ended, and Spartans entered Athens and set up the Thirty Tyrants.

____ Darius II died, and Artaxerxes II became king of Persia.

403 Thirty Tyrants were overthrown in Athens.

401 Cyrus the younger, Artaxerxes II's brother, unsuccessfully revolted to contest the throne by marching eastward from where he was ruling in Asia Minor.

He was supported by 10,000 Greek mercenaries, and was defeated and killed by Persian forces at the Battle of Cunaxa in Mesopotamia. The Greeks were led through Persian territory back to Greece by Xenophon who described the account in his book 'Anabasis'.

399 Socrates died having consented to drink poison.

394 **Spartan fleet was destroyed by a combined Persian and Athenian fleet in the Battle of Cnidus.**

387 **Peace of Antalcidas between Sparta and Persia was established.**

____ Aristophanes, Greek dramatist, died.

384 Aristotle was born.

379 Greek mercenaries gathered to mount a campaign against Egypt.

373 The Greeks' offensive against the native 30th dynasty of Egypt failed.

359 **Artaxerxes II died, and Artaxerxes III became king of Persia.**

356 **Alexander was born.**

350 An attempt by Persians to reclaim Egypt proved futile. This setback encouraged revolt in Sidon and eventually in all of Palestine and Phoenicia.

347 Plato died.

He was the second of the great trio of ancient Greeks (Socrates, Plato, and Aristotle), who between them laid the philosophical foundations of Western culture.

345 **Another attempt by the Persians to reclaim Egypt failed.**

343 **A new wave of offensives on Egypt, led by Artaxerxes III himself, succeeded.**

338 Philip of Macedon, Alexander's father, launched his attack on Greece.

____ Philip became supreme in Greece.

____ **Artaxerxes III was poisoned by his physician upon the order of the eunuch Baogas.**

338 **Baogas made Arses king in hope of becoming the power behind the throne.**
Arses did not condescend easily to Baogas' will.

336 **Arses attempted to poison the kingmaker, Baogas, but was himself killed in retaliation.**
Baogas then engineered the accession of Darius III, a 45-year-old Satrap of Armenia who probably held the closest blood claim to the throne by virtue of being the grandnephew of Artaxerxes II.

336 **Darius III ascended the Achaemenian throne.**

____ **Philip planned an expedition against the Achaemenians.**

335 Aristotle founded his academy and began teaching in Athens.

____ Aristotle began tutoring Alexander.

____ Philip was assassinated and Alexander, having been elected the supreme general of the Greeks, took over command of Philip's army.
Alexander's army consisted of two elements, the Macedonians and the Greeks. The Macedonians were the finest military organization of the time. The Greeks had been forced to join and were prepared by Philip.
Alexander's army might be compared to the one that Napoleon led to Egypt. It had historians, scientists, engineers, surveyors, generals, officers and soldiers.
Alexander had the most capable commanders that any army could wish for. The officers and soldiers were well trained and highly experienced. Alexander's army was an excellent disciplined fighting machine.

334 **Alexander crossed Hellespont, and defeated Darius III's army at Granicus.**
The Persians occupied the far bank of the Granicus River (modern Kocabas, flowing into the Sea of Marmara).
Alexander's shock troops forded the stream and clambered up the bank under a shower of javelins. Alexander followed and charged the generals, who were concentrated in the

left center of the Persian line. Darius III was saved from death by his cavalry commander.

333 **Alexander defeated the Persians again at Issus.**
This was one of the decisive victories by which Alexander conquered the Achaemenian Empire. Issus is a plain on the coast of the Gulf of Iskenderun, in present-day southern Turkey. The Macedonian forces, with an infantry phalanx in the center and cavalry on the sides, approached the army of Darius III, which was drawn up on the opposite bank of the Pinarus River. Alexander led the charge across the river, shattering the Persian left wing before turning against the Greek mercenaries who formed the Persian center. His army in confusion, Darius escaped, but his family was captured.

331 Alexander founded Alexandria.

Babylonia submitted to Alexander.

330 **Alexander gave the Persians the final blow at Gaugamela.**
Attempting to stop Alexander's incursion into the Persian empire, Darius III prepared a battleground on the Plain of Gaugamela, near Arbela (present-day Irbil in northern Iraq), and posted his troops to await Alexander's advance. Darius had the terrain of the prospective battlefield smoothed level so that his many chariots could operate with maximum effectiveness against the Macedonians. His total forces greatly outnumbered those of Alexander. Alexander's well-trained army faced Darius' massive battle line and organized for attack, charging the left of the Persians' line with archers, javelin throwers, and cavalry, while defending against Darius' outflanking cavalry with reserve flank guards. During the combat, so much of Darius' cavalry on his left flank were drawn into the battle that they left the Persian infantry in the center of the battle line exposed. Alexander and his personal cavalry immediately wheeled half left and penetrated this gap and then wheeled again to attack the Persians' flank and rear. At this Darius took

flight, and panic spread through his entire army, which began a headlong retreat while being cut down by the pursuing Greeks.

____ Darius III fled before Alexander, and was later assassinated by two of his own men, Barsantiz and Bessus, who were themselves later executed for betraying their king by order of Alexander.

Alexander and the Seleucids

330 – 247

Seleucids, a dynasty of Macedonian kings that reigned in the Middle East, were established when the empire of Alexander was partitioned among his generals. Their kingdom originally extended eastward from Asia Minor into what is now Pakistan. The Seleucid kingdom had two capitals: Antioch in Syria and Seleucia on the Tigris in Mesopotamia. The Seleucids, Greek in language and culture, encouraged Greek colonists to settle in their domains. Nevertheless, in their autocratic rule they followed the example of their Syrian, Mesopotamian, and Persian predecessors. They were frequently involved in wars with the Ptolemies, another Macedonian dynasty that had established itself in Egypt.

330 **Alexander conquered the Achaemenian Empire.**

____ **Alexander entered Susa.**

330 **Alexander burned Persepolis.**

Alexander became king of Asia as the successor of Darius III. His conquest of the Achaemenian Empire marked the end of Achaemenian greatness and the glory of ancient history.

Persian nobles joined Alexander, and together they brought new order to the world. The Persians penetrated into the political and administrative life of the empire. Alexander appointed Macedonians and Persians as satraps and generals.

____ **Atropates, a Persian, was appointed satrap of Media.**

____ **Phrataphernes, a Persian, was reinstated satrap of Parthia.**

____ **Mithrenes, a Persian, was appointed satrap of Armenia.**

____ **Mithrenes couldn't secure his new post, and Orontes remained satrap.**

Alexander's dream was to bring Macedonians, Greeks and Persians together. His intension was to create a fusion of Hellenes and Persians. Inter-marriage en masse between the Greeks and the Persians was mandated to consolidate Greco-Persian union.

He founded cities called Alexandria mostly in the east of Persia where he had to fight more. The cities, based on Achaemenian garrison towns, were military centers to control the strategic routes.

____ **To encourage the Greco-Persian union, Alexander married Roxane, daughter of the Sogdian Lord.**

327 Alexander conquered India.

323 **Alexander died at 33 in Babylonia.**

Alexander died too young to have time to carry out his plans.

What Alexander established survived his death, and his plans were carried out by his successors.

As conquests continued, capable young men replaced old generals of Philip. Three of the young generals were Ptolemy, Antigonos, and Seleucus. After Alexander's death, his generals sought and declared their independence.

322 Aristotle died.

____ Ptolemy became king of Egypt.

____ Antigonos became king of Media (Atropatene).

____ Seleucus became king of Persia.

312 Seleucus founded the Seleucid dynasty.

311 Seleucus began to quell all opposition in Babylonia and Persia.

Seleucus created a system of military colonies.

Seleucus fought much to secure the allegiance of satraps and local rulers.

He secured the allegiance of Bactria, Media, Macedonia, Syria, Anatolia.

Seleucus re-founded the centers that had declined, such as Ecbatana and Hecatampylus.

305 Seleucus formally became king of Persia.

Hellenism marked the beginning of foreign rule and disunity.

Seleucus introduced the concept of polis and city life and ruled for 25 years. He did well and loyalty to his house remained strong.

His political and military purpose was primarily to ensure his rule. Areas of importance were Egypt, Babylonia, Anatolia, Ionia, and Media, which was a valuable source of horses needed for their cavalry.

Seleucids achieved a uniform currency and monetary system, but Achaemenian institutions like road and post systems remained unchanged.

The great innovation and main function of the Seleucids was founding cities. Seleucus and later Seleucid rulers scattered Greek settlements throughout the empire, but there were not enough Greeks and Macedonians to control all of Asia.

300 Antioch, now in Turkey, was founded by Seleucus Nicator as capital of his Syrian kingdom.

300 Zeno of Citium, founder of Stoicism and Epicurus, founder of Epicureanism, flourished in Athens.

300 Euclid, the most prominent mathematician of Greco-Roman antiquity, flourished. He is best known for his treatise on geometry.

280 Seleucus was assassinated in Greece.

The Greek way of life and practice meant spread of language, law, and culture.

The king was the supreme judge, general, legislator, and nerve center. The court was house of the king and his friends, families, slaves, and servants. There was no national Seleucid state, but subjects of the Seleucid king. The Greeks learned about methods of agriculture, new fruits, and new crops. The Greeks called peaches and oranges 'Persian apples', and 'Median apples'. Imperial and cultural traditions were maintained with little Greek influence. Greeks primarily influenced art, architecture, and religion. Zoroastrianism declined, and cults of Heracles and Mithra were preached.

Hellenization of the Persians led to the Persianization of the Greeks.

Fars established its independence in an uprising against the Seleucids.

250 New centers of power were emerging in Asia Minor.

The Ptolemies ruled in Egypt.

The Kushans, a people of Persian origin, ruled in Bactria.

Parthians, who had migrated from northeast although their origin is uncertain, began to assert their independence.

____ Arsaces, the head of Parni tribe and the vassal of the Bactrian Greeks, revolted and fled westwards to establish his rule.

Parni was one of three nomadic or semi-nomadic tribes in the confederacy of the Dahae living east of the Caspian Sea whose members founded the Parthian empire.

Parthian Period

247 BC – 224 AD

Parthians, subject successively to the Assyrians, Medes, Persians, Macedonians under Alexander, and Seleucids, managed to establish themselves as the Seleucids gradually lost control of the lands east of the Euphrates River and were ultimately expelled from Asia Minor. Being excellent horsemen and archers, the Parthians succeeded in founding an independent kingdom that grew into an empire extending from the Euphrates River to the Indus River and from the Oxus (now Amu Darya) River to the Indian Ocean. After the middle of the 1st century BC, Parthia was a rival of Rome, and several wars occurred between the two powers.

247 Parthians began dating their history.
The Parthians were more pragmatic and less pretentious than the Achaemenians. They were militarily formidable owing to their highly maneuverable cavalry.

____ Daho-Parno-Parthian tribes chose "chiefs for war and princes for peace" from among the closest circle of the princely family. They were famous for their breeding of horses, for their combat cavalry, and for their fine archers.

____ The Parthian language was closely related to Scythian and Median.

____ The Parni, with Arsaces at their head, took the province of Parthia after having defeated Andragoras; soon, neighboring Hyrcania was annexed and the Caspian accessed.

232 Seleucus II arrived in the east to put down the Parthian rebellion.

____ He made peace with Arsaces, who recognized his soverignty.
Arsaces, who had remained closely allied with the nomads to the north, fled to the home of the Scythians. Seleucus decided to cross Jaxartes but having suffered losses at the hands of nomads, and after receiving alarming news from the west, he returned to Syria.

____ Arsaces changed his policy. He no longer acted as a nomad but rather posed as a chief of state, a worthy successor to the Seleucids, whose example he followed.

____ Arsaces crowned himself in the city of Asaak, and the tribe took the name of the Parthians, their close relatives.

____ Arsaces founded the city of Nisa, 18 km (12 miles) northwest of Ashkhabad.

____ Arsaces set up his capital at Hecatampylus, 32 km (20 miles) west of Damghan.

223 Antiochus III became the Seleucid king.

221 The construction of the Great Wall of China began.

212 Archimedes, the Greek mathematician, died.

212 Antiochus III undertook his campaign for recovery of the high satrapies.

211 Arsaces died and his son, Artabanus (Arsaces II), succeeded.

____ Being already solidly established in Parthia and Hyrcania, Artabanus tried to extend his possessions, toward Media.

____ Antiochus III's operations against Artabanus were successful.

He took Hecatampylus and crossed the mountains separating that province from Parthia, which he occupied.

____ Artabanus fled and took refuge with the friendly Scythians, to the north, as had his father, Arsaces I.

____ The conflict was ended by a compromise struck due to the Bactrian uprising.

____ Antiochus III made peace with Artabanus.

____ Antiochus III accorded the title of king to Artabanus, in exchange for recognition of his fealty, and obliged the Parthians to send troops to reinforce the Syrian army.

191 Priapatius succeeded Artabanus.

____ Priapatius' name appears in documents found in excavations at Nisa.

176 Phraates succeeded Priapatius.

____ Once again the young Parthian kingdom resumed expansionist activities.

____ Parthians attacked Media and were successful in the conquest of Mardi tribe near the Caspian.

____ Phraates designated his brother Mithradates as a successor, even though he had several sons.

171 Mithradates assumed the imperial diadem.

____ He opened a new period in the destinies of the kingdom which historians call "phil-Hellinistic" (171 BC-10 AD).

This period was characterized by a strong Hellenistic cultural influence, manifested in the use of the Greek language and in particular in the Arts, although national traditions were not completely abandoned.

____ To show his complete independence, Mithradates minted coins bearing his likeness, wearing a royal diadem like the Seleucid kings.

166 The plague devastated Italy.

155 Mithradates occupied Media.

This opened the route to Mesopotamia.

148 Mithradates reached Ecbatana, where he moved his capital.

____ Rhagae, modern Reyy, south of present-day Tehran, was re-founded and given the dynastic name of Arsacia.

141 Mithradates took Seleucia on the Tigris and was recognized the king of Babylonia.

139 Parthian forces conquered Susiana and Elymais.

138 Phraates II succeeded Mithradates.

____ Phraates II was defeated in several battles by the powerful Seleucid army of Antiochus VII Sidetes.

____ For the last time, Antiochus VII led a Seleucid army to recover Persia.

129 Phraates II defeated Antiochus VII, the last of the Seleucids.

With the arrival of winter, Antiochus quartered his troops in several localities in Media. The local population, exasperated by the undisciplined Syrian soldiery, rose up in revolt. Antiochus was killed and his son taken prisoner. This was a turning point in the history of the eastern Mediterranean with Greco-Macedonian domination receiving a decisive blow which would lead it to its final collapse 46 years later.

128 Phraates II lost his life fighting the revolt of Sakas, a group of Scythian nomads to the north of his frontiers.

____ With some difficulty, Artabanus II, Phraates II's successor and uncle, pushed back Sakas toward Drangiana, to which they gave their name, Sakastan or Sistan.

123 Mithradates II ascended the throne.

____ Mithradates II restored order in its eastern frontiers of Magiana and Aria.

____ **Mithradates II extended his hegemony over Armenia and eastern Asia Minor.**

____ **He exerted military pressure on the last Seleucids.**

92 **A meeting with Rome that had already formed a "Province of Asia" in Asia Minor became inevitable and took place on the Euphrates.**

The two parties recognized the Euphrates as a common frontier.

91 **Mithradates II appointed Gotarzes as satrap of Babylonia.**

Mithradates II and Gotarzes are depicted in the Parthian bas-relief at Bisotun.

____ **For the first time, Parthian power entered into direct contact with the Chinese empire and received an embassy from the Han emperor Wu-ti (r.140-87).**

The Chinese were particularly interested in the horses raised in Fergana, which they needed to create a cavalry to fight the nomadic Hsiung-nu, or Huns, on their northern border.

80 Building of the Colosseum was completed in Rome.

70 **Phraates III became the Parthian king after a short period of intrigue and rivalry that saw the succession, in turn, of Gotarzes, Orodes, and Sanatruces.**

69 **An agreement with the Romans renewed the Euphrates line as a frontier.**

66 **Roman general Pompey succeeded in concluding a real alliance with Phraates III against Pontus and Armenia.**

53 **A conflict with Rome broke out under Orodes II.**

The Roman triumvir Crassus crossed the Euphrates. Orodes II protested and invoked the treaty of friendship in vain. Crassus refused to reply until he arrived at Seleucia on the Tigris. It was a breaking of all the agreements concluded in 69 and 66.

____ **Under the command of general Surenas, the Parthian light and heavy cavalry engaged the Romans in a battle near**

Carrhae. The battle cost Rome seven legions and the lives of Crassus and his son.

Through Surena's brilliant victory the routes to Persia and India were closed to Rome.

____ The Euphrates became not only a political but also a spiritual frontier, no effort at Latinization was possible any longer.

48 With Pompey dead, Caesar was the absolute master of the Roman world.

46 Calendar was reformed by Caesar.

44 Caesar was preparing to avenge Crassus' defeat when he was assassinated by Brutus.

____ The duty of following through on Caesar's project fell to Mark Antony.

____ Having concluded an agreement with Quintus Labienus and anticipating Antony's attack, Parthian commander Pacorus crossed into Syria.

Quintus Labienus was a Roman commander on the side of Caesar's assassins who had gone over to the Parthians.

40 The successes of the two armies were startling; Labienus took all of Asia Minor, Pacorus all of Syria and Palestine.

____ For nearly two years, all of the once Achaemenian western provinces fell to the Parthians.

____ Disagreement between Labienus and Pacorus weakened their power.

39 Labienus was defeated and slain. Asia Minor was recovered by the Romans, and the following year the same fate struck Pacorus and his conquests.

____ The capital was moved to Ctesiphon, where the military camp was transformed into a great metropolis, facing Seleucia across the Tigris.

____ At Nisa, the city was expanded, the royal palaces made larger, and the royal hypogea were enriched with precious pieces of fine Greco-Persian art.

38 Orodes II was assassinated by his son Phraates IV.

36 **Mark Antony began to carry out the revenge Caesar had planned.**
He brought his army to Armenia, through which he planned to enter Media and attack Parthia from the north. But cold weather and Phraates' cavalry combined to force Mark Antony to abandon the fight and retreat to Syria.
Mark Antony attacked Parthian territory of Phraaspa, possibly Takht-e Soleiman, leading an army of 20,000 infantry, 4,000 cavalry and about 8,000 logistics. They were crushed and forced to retreat west of Tigris.

34 **Mark Antony launched another campaign and again suffered heavy losses.**
The battle of Carrhae and Mark Antony's defeat raised Parthia to a major power in the eyes of Rome.

The power struggle between Mark Antony and Octavian began in Rome. This forced Mark Antony to abandon his plans against the Parthians.

31 **Octavian (now Augustus) was triumphant over Mark Antony and became the sole master in Rome.**

30 Mark Antony and Cleopatra committed suicide.

30 **Tiridates II, a pretender to the Parthian throne supported by Rome, obliged Phraates IV to leave Mesopotamia and take refuge with his eastern neighbors, the Scythians, who restored him to power.**

27 **Octavian was inaugurating the imperial period of Roman history.**

20 **A pact was signed allowing the return of Roman prisoners and insignia of the conquered legions in the Battle of Carrhae.**
A new phase began in relations between the two states, marked by the conclusion of a real peace that recognized the Euphrates as a border between them. Phraates IV was dealt with as the sovereign of a great nation. Rome renounced its ambitions in the east, and Augustus inaugurated a policy of respect.

____ **The caravan route to India and China was opened.**

____ **Augustus received ambassadors from the many eastern peoples.**

____ **Armenia remained a source of constant conflict between Parthia and Rome despite apparent resolutions.**
Controlled by Rome, Armenia would be a channel for penetration into Parthia from the north, but controlled by Parthia, it would offer an outlet on the Black Sea, over which Rome asserted its authority. The rivalry of the two powers over this country would remain for centuries a stumbling block to peace.

2 **Phraates V assassinated Phraates IV with his mother's help and assumed the throne.**
He was Phraates IV's son by Musa, a Roman slave girl given to him by Augustus.

____ Jesus Christ (A) was born.

AD

4 **Orodes III succeeded Phraates V.**

7 **The short reign of Orodes III was followed by that of Vonones.** Vonones was Phraates IV's son.

12 **Vonones was driven out by the Parthian nobility whose role at this time became dominant in internal politics and dynastic questions, because of Vonones' Roman habits.**

____ **Vonones' fall brought a change in the destinies of the Empire.**

____ **The anti-Hellenistic period began.**
This period embraces a century and a half (12-162). It is characterized by an expansion of the Parthian national culture and an opposition to all foreign things.

12 **The barons chose Artabanus III to replace Vonones.**
They were certainly mistaken in believing they would find him an easy instrument to manipulate. Artabanus was the

son of a viceroy of Hyrcania and was only Arsacid on his mother's side.

____ **Artabanus III made an abortive attempt to place his son on the throne of Armenia.**

____ **Artabanus III avoided confronting Rome and dedicated himself to internal reforms.**

Among the reforms, centralization occupied the place of first importance. He had to reduce the hereditary privileges the barons had carved out for themselves. It was also necessary to recognize the states that made up the kingdom. He put princes of his family on the various thrones of these states.

____ **Artabanus III made a new attempt to place a son on the throne in Armenia.**

This angered the Romans, who, with the aid of the nobility, sent for Tiridates III. Tiridates III was a pretender the barons had crowned in Ctesiphon. They obliged Artabanus III to take refuge with the Dahae, who helped him win back his throne.

30 Probable date of crucifixion of Jesus Christ (A).

37 **A meeting with a Roman representative on a bridge in the middle of the Euphrates allowed an agreement to be reached that maintained the status quo in Armenia and recognized the Parthian sovereignty with the river as the frontier.**

51 **The throne passed to Vologases, an ardent anti-Roman, after the short reign of Vonones II.**

____ **The Parthian Empire, according to the Roman historian Pliny, was composed of 18 kingdoms, 11 in the north and seven in the south, some governed by Arsacid princes and others by local dynasties.**

51 **A period that showed a slow dissolution of the Parthian state and its disintegration into several small countries, 51-122, began.**

58 **Hyrcania became independent.**

____ Vologases wanted his brother, Tiridates, to be king of Armenia, a desire that put him in the position of a break with Rome, which opposed him militarily.

____ Upon orders from Nero, Corbulo undertook operations which were broken off by the exchange of ambassadors.

64 The Great Fire of Rome, Nero's fire, occurred.

65 First persecution of Christians took place in Rome.

66 An agreement was finally reached. Tiridates left for Rome with his whole family surrounded by a retinue of princes and 3,000 Parthian nobles. He received from Nero the crown of Armenia, and an end to hostilities was announced. This was a clear indication of Parthian political victory over the Romans.

____ Avesta, the holy book of Zoroastrians, was compiled and coins were issued on which, for the first time, Pahlavi characters were added to the Greek legend.

78 Pacorus came to the throne.

80 Pacorus was replaced by the ephemeral Artabanus IV.

81 Artabanus IV was permanently replaced by Pacorus.

____ The country showed signs of a profound decay. The barons refused to obey the crown. In the provinces, the army and finances were in the hands of the nobility. Aristocrats occupied the highest positions, and these positions became hereditary. Plots with Rome were hatched.

109 Pacorus was replaced by Osroes, his brother or brother-in-law.

114 Emperor Trajan invaded Armenia. With Armenia occupied, the Emperor descended with his army into Mesopotamia. All Babylonia was taken and Ctesiphon, the capital, fell into the hands of the Romans, who carried off a daughter of Osroes and the golden throne of the Parthian kings. Victorious Trajan went as far as the Persian Gulf.

____ Parthian reaction was swift. Faced with the gravity of the Roman offensive, all the princes of the royal house, formerly divided by internal strife, united against the invader.

117 At Ctesiphon, Trajan crowned a new vassal king, but revolt was in the wind and attempts to disunite the Parthian chiefs failed.

____ The Romans suffered losses, and Trajan abandoned the campaign and died on his way home.

This put an end to the short-lived Roman victories.

117 Trajan's successor, Hadrian (r.117-138), abandoned all pretensions to Armenia, Mesopotamia, and Assyria.

____ Hadrian's desire for peace seems to have been sincere. He sent back Osroes' daughter, promised to return the Golden throne.

____ 40 years of peace with Rome began.

147 Vologases IV came to the throne.

Although he didn't have to dispute the throne with a pretender during his long reign, underneath the apparent calm the intrigues against him continued, with Rome receiving embassies from the Hyrcanias, the Bactrians, and doubtless from the Kushans.

161 A new clash with Rome came; this time upon the initiative of Vologases IV, who considered himself strong enough to attack.

He occupied Armenia, crossed the Euphrates, and invaded Syria, which had not seen Parthian cavalry for two centuries. The Syrian population, which included Jews driven from Palestine by the Romans, received the Parthians as liberators although the country had been Roman since the time of Pompey,

____ The situation became so serious that Lucius Verus, co-emperor with Marcus Aurelius, was dispatched to the east with strong reinforcement taken from the fronts on the Danube and Rhine.

163 The Romans re-took Armenia and succeeded in a campaign similar to that of Trajan's.

164 Ctesiphon fell to the Romans, who razed the royal palace. But once more success was transitory.

The Roman army had come from Armenia and crossed through Azerbaijan, where plague was endemic. Contaminated, the Roman army was sorely fatigued by disease and obliged to retreat, but not definitively. Lucius Verus, repeating his campaigns in Armenia and northern Mesopotamia, inflicted heavy losses on the Parthians.

193 Septimius Severus became emperor. He began operations that permitted him to occupy first northern and then southern Mesopotamia and, for the third time in a century, Ctesiphon.

____ The Parthians in their retreat adopted a scorched-earth policy.

As under Trajan, the starving Roman army went back up the Tigris, failed in its attempt to take Hatra, and left the country.

208 Ardashir, satrap of Pars, began to establish regional authority.

Pars territory consisted of several tribal monarchies, one of which lay between Pasargadae and Persepolis at Istakhr, where Papak, Ardashir's father, was the keeper of Adur-Anahid, or Anahid Fire Temple.

208 Vologases VI, son of the former Parthian king, succeeded him.

213 Artabanus V, a Parthian prince, started contesting the throne of Vologases VI, with the help of the king of Media.

213 The Arsacid Empire became divided between Vologases VI (r.208-222), who seems to have ruled in Ctesiphon on the left bank of the middle Tigris in what is now Iraq, and Artabanus V (r.213-224), who was in control of Persia and whose authority at Susa is attested by an inscription of 215 AD.

_____ **A new invasion of Mesopotamia took place under Caracalla, the casus belli being the refusal of Artabanus V to give Caracalla his daughter in marriage.**

The young Roman emperor dreamed of rebuilding Alexander's empire but succeeded only in the pillage of Media and destruction at Arbela of the hypogea of the Arsacid kings, whose bones he scattered.

_____ **The Parthian reply was harsh. Artabanus V avenged himself by invading the Roman provinces and destroying several cities.**

Rome sued for peace. Artabanus' conditions were too stringent and were refused. Hostilities were taken up again and turned in favor of the Parthians who obtained such a success that the emperor Marcinus paid 200,000,000 sesterces to make peace.

216 **Mani, or Manes, the founder of Manichaeism and the second great prophet of pre-Islamic Persia, was born on April 14 near Ctesiphon.**

His father, Patek, a native of Hamadan, had joined a religious community practicing baptism and abstinence. Mani's mother was related to the Parthian royal family.

_____ **As a boy Mani saw in vision an angel.**

224 **Ardashir narrowed his opponents to one, Artabanus V.**

The process of decentralization and weakening had already started in Parthian territory, and satraps had begun to revolt. It was inevitable that one of the revolts would succeed.

Success came to the ruler of Persis or Pars, Ardashir.

_____ **Ardashir and Artabanus V left their armies aside and met at the battle of Hormizdgan in a hand-to-hand combat.**

_____ **Standing over the corpse of his rival, Ardashir claimed the title of king of kings.**

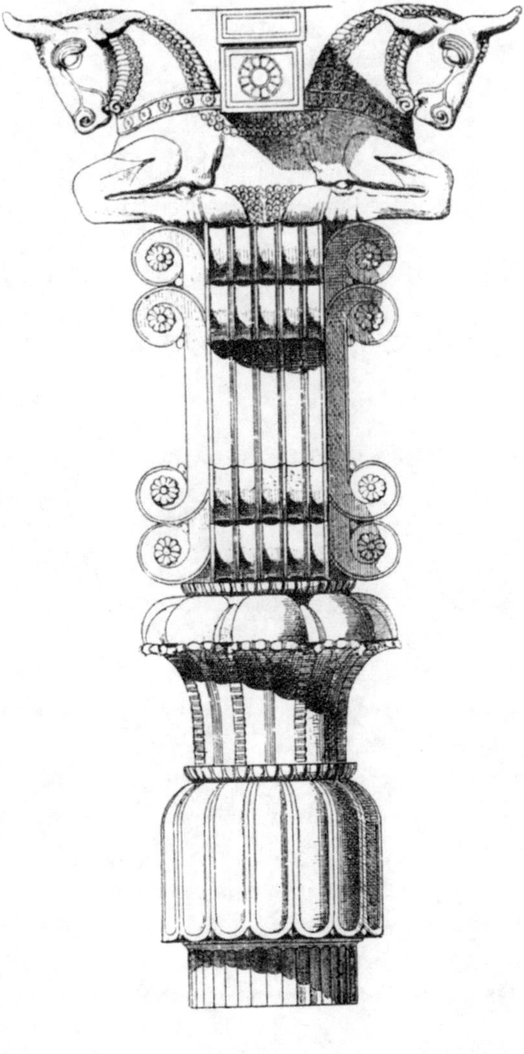

Sassanian Period

224 – 642

Sassanians, an Iranian dynasty evolved by Ardashir I, overthrew the Parthians and created an empire that was constantly changing in size as it reacted to Rome and Byzantium to the west and to the Kushans and Hephthalites to the east. Under Sassanian rule a revival of Iranian nationalism took place, and Zoroastrianism became the state religion. The government was centralized with provincial officials directly responsible to the throne. Financed by the government, Iranian art and architecture experienced a general renaissance, metalwork and gem engraving became highly sophisticated, agriculture developed, scholarship was encouraged, and works from both the East and West were translated into Pahlavi, the language of the Sassanians.

224 Ardashir founded the Sassanian Empire and became king of Persia.

The ancestors of Ardashir had played a leading role in the rites of the fire temple at Istakhr. With the new dynasty having these priestly antecedents, important developments in the Zoroastrian religion occurred during the Sassanian period.

____ Ardashir extended his military and political victories by taking possession of the palace in Ctesiphon; by his assuming the title "king of kings of the Iranians"; and by his re-founding and re-building of the city of Seleucia, located on the Tigris under the new name of Weh-Ardashir ("the Good Deed of Ardashir").

____ Kartir, an influential high priest of Zoroastrianism, flourished. His aim was to purge Persia of all other religions, especially Manichaeism. He retained his position in the Sassanian court for half a century up to the reign of Bahram I, when he died.

240 For the second time, Mani beheld in vision an angel calling him to preach a new religion at the age of 24.

Mani obeyed the heavenly order to manifest himself publicly and to proclaim his doctrines. He combined the doctrines of Zoroaster, Buddha and Jesus (A) to introduce a new religion of a universal character.

____ Mani traveled to India, probably Sind and Turan, and made converts.

240 Ardashir abdicated the throne in favor of his chosen heir, his son Shapur.

Shapur assumed the responsibilities of government but delayed his coronation until after his father's death.

241 Shapur crowned himself assuming the title of "king of kings of Iran and non-Iran".

____ Christianity gained a firm footing in the lands of Tigris and Euphrates.

As long as the Roman Empire remained pagan, the Christian communities of Persia lived undisturbed by persecution.

241 **Mani was favorably received on his return by the newly crowned Persian king, Shapur.**

Mani was permitted to preach his religion in the Persian Empire during the long reign of Shapur.

Mani presented the king with his first book, the "Shapuregan", ("dedicated to Shapur"), a summary of his teachings written in the Middle Persian language.

To him, the essence of all religions was the Truth, and that existence was a constant battle between Good—offering peaceful harmony—and Evil, causing constant agitation. Good and Evil manifested themselves in the individual in separation of body and soul, heart and mind, sensual and spiritual. In society, this duality reflected itself in the conflict between 'divine' spiritualism and 'satanic' spiritualism. His religious philosophy appealed to many in Persia, Central Asia, China, Syria, North Africa and Italy.

244 **The Emperor Gordian levied across the Roman Empire an army of Goths and Germans against Persia. On the border of Asuristan at Massice ("Misikhe" on the Euphrates), a great battle took place. The emperor Gordian was killed and the Roman army destroyed.**

244 **The Romans proclaimed Philip the Arab emperor.**

Emperor Philip came to peace terms and as ransom for the lives of the Romans, he gave Shapur 500,000 Dinars and became his tributary.

249 Emperor Philip died.

253 Valerian became Emperor.

260 **Emperor Valerian was defeated and captured by the Persians at the battle of Edessa.**

Shapur brought more than 70,000 Roman soldiers to Persia. Rome witnessed the so-called Thirty Tyrants general disorder and revolt.

____ In the northeast Shapur secured the submission of the Kushans.

260 Established priests judged that Mani posed a threat to their power.

266 Odenathus, after raising Palmyra to a position of power and repelling the Persians, was murdered. His widow, Zenobia, became ruler of Palmyra on behalf of her son and made extensive conquests.

272 Shapur died. He was succeeded by his two sons, Hormuz and Bahram, of whose reigns little is known.

274 Under the reign of Bahram, Mani was attacked by Zoroastrian priests and was imprisoned by the king at Gundeshapur.

After 26 days of trials, which his followers called the "Passion of the Illuminator" or Mani's "crucifixion," Mani delivered a final message to his disciples and died sometime between 274 and 277.

276 Bahram II became king and ruled for seventeen years.

____ Bahram II and later Narseh concluded two agreements with the Romans as the result of which the Empire lost its western provinces.

282 Emperor Carus (r.282-283) invaded Mesopotamia without meeting opposition and reached Ctesiphon. His sudden death, however, caused the Roman army to withdraw.

____ Bahram II had been prevented from meeting the Roman challenge by the rebellion of his brother, Hormuz, the ruler of Kushans, who tried to establish an independent eastern empire. This attempt ended in failure, and Bahram II appointed his younger son the future Bahram III, as viceroy of Sakastan, or Sistan.

293 Bahram II died, and Narseh, the youngest son of Shapur, challenged the succession of Bahram III and won the crown.

294 King Tiridates of Armenia adopted the Christian faith, thus Christianity became predominant in Armenia.

296 Narseh was forced to sign a peace treaty with the Romans by which Armenia remained under Roman suzerainty and certain areas in Northern Mesopotamia were ceded to Rome.

By this treaty, which lasted for about 40 years, the Sassanians withdrew completely from the disputed districts.

306 Constantine the Great became the Emperor of Rome. He made Christianity the official religion of the Roman world.

____ The Syro-Christian populations of Mesopotamia and Babylonia began to feel sympathy with Roman policies for religious reasons.

____ Emperor Constantine and Armenia developed closer ties based on their common faith.

Armenia was torn between two factions of its population. Opposed to the newly converted pro-Roman Christians, there was a powerful section of Armenian nobility who maintained the old ties and connections with Persia. The Christian subjects of the king of kings gradually became political suspects in the eyes of the Persian authorities.

309 Shapur II ascended the throne and ruled for seventy years.

For about half a century, Shapur II continued victories over the Romans.

330 Constantinople was founded by Constantine I.

337 Shapur II resumed the war in the west.

He began his assaults with a view to wiping out the disgrace of the two agreements concluded by Bahram II and Narseh with the Romans.

____ The subsequent peace restored the disputed provinces including Armenia to Shapur II.

337 Constantine the Great died.

337 Shapur II began a new war with Rome.

Shapur II besieged the fortress city of Nisibis three times without success.

339 The Sassanian emperors consequently felt the need to consolidate Zoroastrianism, and efforts were made to perfect and enforce state orthodoxy.

All heresy was proscribed by the state, defection from the official faith was made a capital crime, and persecution of the heterodox—the Christians in particular—began.

348 Shapur II defeated the Romans at the battle of Singara.

350 Shapur II was unsuccessful in his third attempt to siege Nisibis.

353 Shapur II was distracted by the appearance of a new enemy, the nomadic Chionites (Huns), on his eastern frontier until 358.

359 Having subjected the Chionites, Shapur II returned to Mesopotamia and with their help captured the city of Amida, modern Diyarbakir, on the upper Tigris.

361 Emperor Julian the Apostate (r.361-363) re-opened hostilities against the Sassanians after the death of Constantius.

Emperor Julian restored paganism.

363 Having reached the vicinity of Ctesiphon, Julian was struck dead with an arrow shot by an unknown party whilst negotiating with Shapur II.

Julian was succeeded by Jovian.

363 Emperor Jovian was forced to give up the Roman possessions on the Tigris, including Nisibis, and to abandon Armenia and his Arsacid protégé, Arsaces III, to the Sassanians.

The greater part of Armenia then became a Persian province.

Emperor Jovian signed a humiliating peace treaty with the Sassanians.

364 Emperor Valentinian divided the Roman Empire into eastern and western Empires, and appointed Valens as the eastern Emperor.

379 Shapur II died.

His death was followed by half a century of decline in the power of the kings.

____ Ardashir II, Shapur III, Bahram IV took their turn on the Sassanian throne.

399 Yazdgerd came to the throne.

His initial inclination toward tolerance of the Christian and Jewish religions was met by resistance on the part of nobility.

420 Yazdgerd died.

____ **The nobles refused to admit any of Yazdgerd's sons to the throne.**

421 **Despite the nobles refusal, a son of Yazdgerd, Bahram V eventually won the throne.**

Bahram V, or Bahram Gur ("Hunter of Onager"), became a favorite of Persian popular tradition exuberantly celebrating his prowess in hunting and love. He was also renowned as a poet and musician.

422 **Unsuccessful in war against the Romans, Bahram V made a 100-year peace and granted freedom of worship to the Christians.**

____ **In the east Bahram V succeeded in repelling an invasion by a new wave of Hephthalites.**

According to Chinese chronicles, Hephthalites were originally a tribe living to the north of the Great Wall. Elsewhere they were called White Huns or Hunas. They had no cities or system of writing, lived in felt tents, and practiced polyandry. Nothing is known of their language.

422 **Eastern Empire launched successful campaigns against Persia.**

____ **Bahram V fought a short war with Byzantium.**

The war ended in an agreement because Bahram did not believe in oppressing Christians. The new entente between Rome and Persia led to freedom of worship for the Christians.

438 **Bahram V died and was succeeded by Yazdgerd II.**

After his death, another century of upheaval shook the Sassanian Empire.

457 King Piruz ascended the Sassanian throne.

____ Piruz fell in battle with the Hephthalites; his treasure and family were captured, and the country was devastated.

484 King Balash, Piruz's brother, became king.

486 King Balash, unable to cope with continuing incursions, was deposed and blinded.

488 King Kavad ruled his first reign for eight years.

488 The crown fell to Kavad, or Qobad, son of Piruz.

490 Mazdak propagated his theology.

Mazdakism was the second heresy to strike the theocratic Sassanian state.

At this time Persia was ravaged by famine, drought, military defeat, epidemic of plague and social disorder.

496 While the empire continued to suffer distress, Kavad was dethroned and imprisoned.

499 Kavad escaped to the Hephthalites and with their assistance was restored to the throne for the second time.

____ The Nestorian doctrine claiming that divine and human persons remained separate in the incarnate Christ had by then become dominant among the Christians in Persia and was definitely established as the accepted form of Christianity in the Empire.

____ Kavad proved himself a vigorous ruler and restored peace and order in the land.

502 Roman Empire and Persia fought a battle that lasted five years.

The campaign against the Romans resulted in the destruction of Amida, but another inroad by the Hephthalites in the east compelled Kavad to ratify a peace treaty with Byzantines.

522 Another war took place between the Romans and the Persians.

524 Mazdak was assassinated as a result of the intrigue of the Zoroastrian priesthood.

527 Kavad resumed the war and defeated the Byzantine general Belisarius.

528 The crown prince Khosrow, who was an Orthodox Zoroastrian, in collaboration with the chief magus, plotted the condemnation of the Mazdakites and their massacre.

531 Khosrow Anushirvan became king and introduced extensive reforms.

Under Khosrow, the empire reached its zenith. Khosrow in particular favored extensive irrigation and urbanism. Villages were rebuilt, roads and bridges restored, and neglected canals cleaned out. Khosrow had the myths and stories of heroes collected. The famous Persian carpet 'Spring of Khosrow' was woven. Khosrow's reputation as an enlightened and just ruler was celebrated during his lifetime and later became legendary.

____ Khosrow re-established Zoroastrian orthodoxy.

Khosrow's authority was recognized by all classes including priesthood.

____ Khosrow re-established Persia as a military power.

Compulsory military service was introduced.

532 A peace treaty was concluded between Justinian and Khosrow.

The restoration of peace brought about a considerable amount of religious tolerance, especially towards Christians.

____ Khosrow moved the capital to Ctesiphon.

Administration of government was organized on a hierarchical basis and society was differentiated into clearly defined social classes.

____ A new imperial tax system was established.

The levying of land revenue in kind was replaced by a fixed assessment in cash.

540 Khosrow began his long military campaigns against Justinian, with the invasion of Syria.

541 Khosrow extended his power to the Black Sea and inflicted heavy defeats on the Hephthalites.

He burned Antioch and transplanted many of its inhabitants to a new town already built on the same plan near Ctesiphon.

542 The plague devastated Europe.

560 A new nation, that of the Turks, emerged in the east.

By concluding an alliance with a Turkish leader called Sinjibu (Silzibul), Khosrow was able to inflict a decisive defeat on the Hephthalites.

562 Another peace treaty was concluded between Justinian and Khosrow.

562 Khosrow had all the followers of Mazdak purged in one day.

Neither Mazdakism nor Manichaeism totally died in Persia.

565 Emperor Justinian died.

570 Abul Qasim Mohammad Ibn Abdullah Ibn Abdul Mutallib Ibn Hashim (S) was born in Mecca after the death of his father.

He later became the Prophet of Islam, the last in the line of the Old and New Testament Prophets according to the Qur'an.

____ Mohammad (S) went under the care of his paternal grandfather Abdul Mutallib, the head of the prestigious Hashim clan and a prominent figure in Mecca politics.

Mecca, inhabited by the tribe of Quraysh, to which the Hashim clan belonged, was a mercantile center formed around a sanctuary, the Kaaba, which assured the safety of those who came to trade at the fairs.

Mecca was strategically located on a trade route between Yemen and the Mediterranean region. Goods were carried on this trade route from India and Ethiopia to the Mediterranean area—Gaza and Damascus.

572 There was a renewal of war between Persia and the Roman Empire.

The alliance between Khosrow and the Turks became a source of friction during this war. The Turks sometimes acted as ally of Byzantium against Persia.

573 Abu Bakr, who later became the first Caliph, was born.

575 The Persians conquered Yemen in Arabia.

576 Mohammad (S) lost his mother, Amina of the clan of Zuhra.

578 Mohammad (S) lost his grandfather and came under the care of the new head of the clan, his uncle Abu Talib.

By Arab custom, minors did not inherit; therefore, Mohammad (S) did not have a share in the property of his father and grandfather. Mohammad (S) accompanied his uncle on trading journeys to Syria.

579 Khosrow bequeathed the war to his son Hormuz IV (579-590) who in spite of repeated negotiations failed to re-establish peace between Byzantium and Persia.

Hormuz IV was unable to display the same authority as his father, and antagonized the Zoroastrian clergy by failing to take action against the Christians.

586 Umar Ibn al-Khattab, who later became the second Caliph, was born.

590 Bahram Chubin led a military coup against Hormuz IV.

Bahram Chubin was an outstanding military figure and was not a member of the Sassanian family. He dethroned Hormuz IV with the support of the nobles and the army.

590 The last great king of Sassanians, Khosrow II (Khosrow Parviz), ascended the throne.

Khosrow II was the grandson of Khosrow Anushirvan.

Bahram Chubin seized the capital and declared himself king.

Khosrow II was compelled to take refuge with the Emperor Maurice from whom he obtained troops.

Byzantium exacted a heavy price for this assistance and Persia lost practically all Armenia.

591 Bahram Chubin, routed by Khosrow II, fled and was killed by the Turks. This marked the beginning of Khosrow II's reign.

595 Mohammad (S) married Khadija (R).
He had been in charge of the business tradings of Khadija, a rich woman from the clan of Asad. The 40-year-old Khadija was so impressed by Mohammad (S) that she proposed marriage, which proved a turning point in Mohammad (S)'s life.

600 Ali Ibn Abu Talib (A) was born in Mecca.

602 Sassanian armies entered Byzantium.

602 Mu'awiya the son of Abu Sufyan, was born.
He later became the founder of the Umayyad dynasty in 661.

602 The assassination of Maurice gave Khosrow II the pretext he needed to attack Byzantium.

____ Khosrow II's army penetrated as far as Chalcedon, opposite Constantinople.

605 Fatima (A), the Prophet (S)'s daughter, was born.

610 Reflecting in Hera, a cave near Mecca, Mohammad (S) received the divine revelation.
The revelations, disclosed to him through the intermediary of the Archangel Gabriel, commanded the Prophet (S) to recite in the name of God, which marked the beginning of his mission as the messenger of God.
At frequent intervals until his death, he received revelations directly from God. The revelations proclaimed a new religious and social order based on allegiance to one god, and became the cornerstone of Muslim faith, practice and law.
As asserted in the Qur'an, Mohammad (S) is neither a divinity nor a figure of worship, but merely a human to whom revelations are disclosed.

610 Ten-year-old Ali (A) became one of the first converts to Islam.

611 The Persian army captured Antioch and Damascus.

613 Prophet Mohammad (S) began preaching publicly.

614 Sassanians conquered Jerusalem and brought part of the True Cross to Ctesiphon.

614 Aisha, Abu Bakr's daughter and a future wife of the Prophet (S), was born.

615 Active opposition appeared against Prophet Mohammad (S) and his teachings.

Although his preaching was basically religious, it criticized the conduct and attitudes of the rich merchants of Mecca. Certain points in the Qur'an were questioned. According to the available information, commercial pressure was brought on his supporters numbering seventy. They were mostly young men, sons and brothers of the richest men in Mecca, when they joined Mohammad (S).

615 The persecution led to the emigration of some of the Muslims to Ethiopia.

616 Sassanians conquered Sardis and Ephesus.

616 The chief clans of Mecca boycotted the clan of Hashim for continuing to support Mohammad (S) and not curbing his preaching.

The Prophet (S) and his followers were forced to retreat to the She'b of Abu Talib, a valley near Mecca, where they were compelled to stay for three years.

619 Khadija, who remained the sole spouse of the Prophet (S) until then, died at the She'b of Abu Talib, leaving the Prophet (S) in great grief.

619 Abu Talib, full brother of the Prophet (S)'s father, died. Although he protected the Prophet (S), he never converted to Islam.

619 Abu Lahab, uncle of Prophet Mohammad (S), succeeded as head of Hashim clan.

619 The boycott against Hashim clan lost momentum.

Perhaps because some of the participants realized they were harming their own economic interests.

619 Abu Lahab, closer to the richest merchants and at their instigation, withdrew the protection of the clan, or the Right of Javar, from Mohammad (S).
This made Prophet Mohammad (S) vulnerable to attack, which undermined his ability to propagate his religion in Mecca.

619 Mohammad (S) left for the neighboring town of at-Ta'if.
The inhabitants were unprepared to receive his message and he failed to find support. Having secured the protection of the head of another clan, he returned to Mecca.

619 Sassanian army occupied Egypt.
The Byzantine Empire was indeed at its lowest ebb.

620 Persia pushed Byzantium all the way back to Constantinople.
Persia regained frontiers it had not held since the time of Achaemenians.

621 Mohammad (S) married Aisha whom he held most dear.
This enhanced Abu Bakr's prominence in the early Muslim community.

621 Twelve men from Medina, visiting Mecca for the annual pilgrimage to the Kaaba, still a pagan shrine, secretly professed themselves Muslims to Prophet Mohammad (S).
They went back to propagate the new theology in Medina.

622 Having rebuilt the nucleus of a new army since his coronation in 610, Emperor Heraclius set out and retaliated vigorously against the Persians.

622 A representative party of 75 persons from Medina, including two women, not merely professed Islam but also took an oath to defend Prophet Mohammad (S) as they would their own kin.

622 Prophet Mohammad (S) encouraged his faithful Meccan followers to make their way to Medina in small groups; about 70 emigrated.

622 Prophet Mohammad (S) decided to migrate to Medina himself.

He chose Abu Bakr as his sole companion on the journey.

622 Meccans plotted to kill Mohammad (S) before he could leave. Ali (A) risked his own life by sleeping in the Prophet (S)'s bed that night to impersonate him so that Prophet Mohammad (S) could slip away unperceived by using unfrequented paths to Medina.

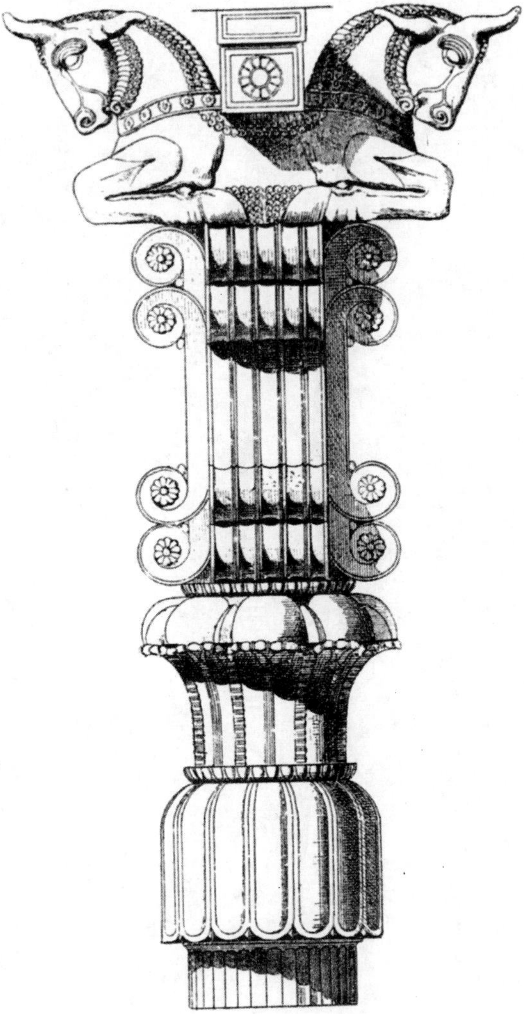

Advent of Islam

642 – 661

The third decade of the seventh century was the major turning point in Iranian history, in which the pattern of the country's religious, cultural and psychological development was determined up to the present age. The Arab conquest permeated far deeper into the structure of Iranian civilization than any other before or since. It provided the country with a new religion and a new script; it influenced its language and revolutionized its art. Yet it did not destroy utterly or absorb completely; what was indigenous in Iranian character and customs was driven underground and emerged in new and complex forms.

622 Prophet Mohammad (S) arrived in Medina safely.
This is the celebrated Hegira, or Emigration, the traditional commencement of Islamic history.

____ Prophet Mohammad (S) was given a piece of land and had a house built.

623 Imam Ali (A) married Fatima (A), who bore him two sons, Hassan (A) and Hossein (A), and two daughters, Zainab (A) and Umm-i Kulthum (A).

624 A revelation bade Muslims to face Mecca in prayer instead of Jerusalem.

624 The enlarged house of Prophet Mohammad (S) in Medina was built serving as the primordial mosque of Islam.
Buildings in Arabia were simple structures built of sun-dried mud bricks around a central open courtyard with porches made of palm tree trunks with thatched roofs of palm fronds. It is generally believed that the house of the Prophet must have had the same type of plan.
Certain features of this house remained inseparable to all later mosques: the praying space for communal prayer, the direction of Mecca (the Qibla) so that the worshippers would know which way to face for prayer, and a shelter in the form of a columned space (hypostyle) to protect the worshipers from the elements.

____ The first 18 months after Hegira were spent in settling down.

624 Muslims in Medina depended for economic survival on constant raids on Meccan caravans.

____ A small band of men was sent eastward with sealed orders by Prophet Mohammad (S) telling them to proceed to Nakhla, near Mecca, and attack a caravan from Yemen.
The successful raid made Meccans aware of the seriousness of the threat from Muslims.

624 Hassan (A), Imam Ali (A) and Fatima (A)'s elder son, was born.
Shias considered him to be the second Imam after Ali (A).

624 **Battle of Badr was fought.**
When word of a particularly wealthy caravan, escorted by Abu Sufyan, head of the Umayyad clan, reached Prophet Mohammad (S), he organized a raiding party of 300 Muslims. Having the wells on the caravan route near Medina filled with sand, the Muslims lured Abu Sufyan's army to battle at Badr. Despite the superiority of Meccan forces numbering 1,000, the Muslims scored a complete victory, killing many prominent Meccans.

625 **Battle of Uhud was fought.**
Abu Sufyan mobilized Meccan power, and entered the oasis of Medina with 3,000 men on March 21.
Prophet Mohammad (S) and his 1,000 men confronted Abu Sufyan's army at the hill of Uhud near Medina. On the morning of 23 March the Meccan infantry attacked and was repulsed with considerable loss. As the Muslims pursued, the Meccan cavalry launched a flank attack after the archers guarding the Muslim left flank had abandoned their position. The Muslims were thrown into confusion. Finally, the battle produced neither a clear victor nor a loser.

625 **Mohammad (S) married Umar's daughter, Hafsa.**
This elevated Umar's status among the Muslims.

626 **Hossein (A), the younger son of Imam Ali (A) and Fatima (A), was born in Medina.**
He is revered by Shia Muslims as the third Imam.

____ **Romans attacked Persia throwing Ctesiphon into panic.**

____ **The Persian king fled.**

627 **Battle of the Ditch, or Khandaq, was fought.**
Abu Sufyan led a great confederacy of 10,000 men against Medina. Prophet Mohammad (S) resorted to tactics unfamiliar to the Muslims who were accustomed to brief, isolated raids. Rather than sally out to meet the enemy in the usual way, he had a ditch dug around Medina at the suggestion of his military advisor and companion, Salman Farsi. All attempts to cross the ditch failed while the

Prophet (S)'s agents among the attackers fomented dissension. A night of wind and rain dealt the great Meccan army the final blow and the insurgents melted away.

____ The Prophet (S)'s position was now greatly strengthened owing to his triumph over the Meccans despite all their military superiority.

627 Heraclius entered the Tigris provinces.

628 Khosrow II attempted no resistance, triggering a revolt in which Khosrow II was slain in Ctesiphon by his son Kavad who replaced him.

This marked the beginning of the end of the Sassanian Empire.

628 Kavad II died and anarchy resulted.

____ Heraclius returned the relic of the True Cross to Jerusalem.

628 After a dream, Prophet Mohammad (S) set out on his pilgrimage to Mecca.

He and his accompanying followers, about 1600 men, were forced by the Meccans to halt on the edge of the sacred territory of Mecca, at al-Hudaybiyya. After some critical days the Meccans made a treaty with Prophet Mohammad (S). Hostilities were to cease, and Muslims were allowed to make the pilgrimage to Mecca in 629.

____ Prophet Mohammad (S)'s successful policies were leading more men to become Muslim, and thus his power was growing.

629 An attack by Meccan coalition upon allies of the Prophet (S) led to the condemnation of the treaty of al-Hudaybiyya.

630 Mecca was conquered.

After secret preparations, Prophet Mohammad (S) marched on Mecca with 10,000 men. Abu Sufyan and other leading members went out to meet him and formally submitted, and Prophet Mohammad (S) promised a general amnesty. When he entered Mecca there was virtually no resistance. Two Muslims and 28 of the enemy were killed. Prophet Mohammad (S), who had left Mecca as a persecuted

Prophet (S), not merely entered it again in triumph but also gained the allegiance of most of the Meccans. Though he did not insist on their conversion, many soon did convert. After his victory, Prophet Mohammad (S) soon returned to Medina.

____ **Prophet Mohammad (S) was now militarily the strongest man in Arabia. Most tribes sent deputations to Medina seeking alliance.**

630 **Having at first opposed Prophet Mohammad (S), Abu Sufyan submitted to Islam.**

His daughter, Umm-i Habiba, was married to the Prophet (S).

The first Umayyad Caliph, Mu'awiya, was one of his sons.

630 **Al-Abbas Ibn Abdul Mutallib (died in 653) half-brother of the Prophet (S)'s father Abdullah, joined Prophet Mohammad (S).**

The later Abbasid dynasty, being descended from his son Abdullah Ibn Abbas, were named after him.

630 **Prophet Mohammad (S) pioneered the invasion of Syria, then part of Byzantine Empire.**

He took 30,000 men on a month's journey to the Syrian border, and made agreements that set a precedent for treaty arrangements with captured people.

631 **Mohammad (S) chose Abu Bakr to conduct the public pilgrimage to Mecca.**

632 **Prophet Mohammad (S) personally led the 'farewell pilgrimage' to Mecca, in March.**

Shias believe that the Prophet (S) unequivocally nominated Imam Ali (A) as his successor while he was returning from the 'farewell pilgrimage' to Mecca. Sunnis reject this claim, maintaining that Prophet Mohammad (S) died without naming a successor.

632 **After Ardeshir III and Khosrow III, Yazdgerd III was chosen King.**

____ Yazdgerd III continued Khosrow' work of collecting the stories of heroes.

He appointed Dehghan Daneshvar to update the heroic stories.

He was a senior historian from the imperial court. The term Dehqan was a title that meant 'farmer' as well as 'historian'. He composed Khodaynameh in New Pahlavi language. It consisted of all the heroic tales from the time of Kiyumars to Khosrow II. It became the main source for the future books of Shahnameh.

632 Prophet Mohammad (S) passed away in Medina in June.

Rashidin Caliphs succeeded Prophet Mohammad (S).

Under the Caliphs, Muslim armies brought the new faith to the world.

Meanwhile, the Sassanians had suffered a recurrent series of crises. Centuries of foreign wars and struggles had exhausted them. The empire had expanded and so had the bureaucracy. The central authority of Sassanian court had declined in favor of its generals, who were now ruling the empire. Due to internal crisis, there was no army powerful enough to resist enemy onslaught. The Sassanian administration was about to fall victim to the highly inspired Muslims.

632 Prophet Mohammad (S)'s death thrust the young Muslim community into a protracted debate over the criteria of legitimate succession.

____ Two predominant solutions to the problem of succession emerged. One group maintained that the Prophet (S) had explicitly designated his son-in-law Ali (A) as his successor. The other, convinced that Prophet Mohammad (S) had made no such appointment, opted for consensus to choose from among a group of elder companions of Prophet Mohammad (S). They chose Prophet Mohammad (S)'s father-in-law Abu Bakr as the first Khalifat Rasul Allah ("

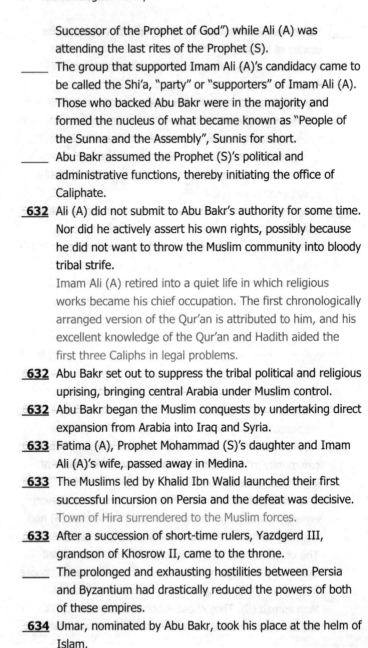

Successor of the Prophet of God") while Ali (A) was attending the last rites of the Prophet (S).

_____ The group that supported Imam Ali (A)'s candidacy came to be called the Shi'a, "party" or "supporters" of Imam Ali (A). Those who backed Abu Bakr were in the majority and formed the nucleus of what became known as "People of the Sunna and the Assembly", Sunnis for short.

_____ Abu Bakr assumed the Prophet (S)'s political and administrative functions, thereby initiating the office of Caliphate.

632 Ali (A) did not submit to Abu Bakr's authority for some time. Nor did he actively assert his own rights, possibly because he did not want to throw the Muslim community into bloody tribal strife.

Imam Ali (A) retired into a quiet life in which religious works became his chief occupation. The first chronologically arranged version of the Qur'an is attributed to him, and his excellent knowledge of the Qur'an and Hadith aided the first three Caliphs in legal problems.

632 Abu Bakr set out to suppress the tribal political and religious uprising, bringing central Arabia under Muslim control.

632 Abu Bakr began the Muslim conquests by undertaking direct expansion from Arabia into Iraq and Syria.

633 Fatima (A), Prophet Mohammad (S)'s daughter and Imam Ali (A)'s wife, passed away in Medina.

633 The Muslims led by Khalid Ibn Walid launched their first successful incursion on Persia and the defeat was decisive. Town of Hira surrendered to the Muslim forces.

633 After a succession of short-time rulers, Yazdgerd III, grandson of Khosrow II, came to the throne.

_____ The prolonged and exhausting hostilities between Persia and Byzantium had drastically reduced the powers of both of these empires.

634 Umar, nominated by Abu Bakr, took his place at the helm of Islam.

Umar's reign saw the transformation of the Islamic state from an Arabian principality to a world power. Under Umar, Muslim armies conquered Mesopotamia and Syria and began the conquest of Persia and Egypt.

____ Muslim troops pushed toward Syria and Byzantium surrendered.

____ Army commander Abu Ubaida was defeated in a battle against the Persians.

635 Muthni Ibn Haritha defeated the Sassanians in the third battle.

636 Sa'd Ibn Waqqas severely defeated the Persians at the battle of Qadisiyya.

____ Commander Rostam Farrokhzad was killed at the battle of Qadisiyya.

637 Low lands of Iraq submitted to the Muslims.

Commander Hormozan resisted for 21 years in Ahvaz and Shushtar.

638 Ctesiphon fell to the vigorous Muslim campaign.

640 Mu'awiya was appointed governor of Damascus by Caliph Umar.

641 Luqman Ibn Muqran commanded the invading forces at Nehavand, western Persia.

____ Sassanians were decisively defeated at the battle of Nehavand.

642 Yazdgerd III was defeated and his heirs fled to China.

The splendid and gigantic edifice of the Sassanians crumbled to pieces. Within a decade, the proud period of Sassanian rule came to a close.

Muslims Conquest of Persia

642 Muslims peacefully occupied Persia.

Persians welcomed the deliverance promised by the invaders.

Cities that resisted such as Reyy, Susa and Sarakhs were conquered by force of arms.

644 Umar, the second Caliph, was killed by Abu Lo'lo, a Christian Persian slave, and Uthman succeeded him as third Caliph.

Choice of Uthman over Imam Ali (A) stirred waves of discontent within the community of Muslims. As Uthman took over control, some Muslims designated themselves as Shia of Imam Ali (A)—supporter of Imam Ali (A)—who was continuing to live in the simple manner of Prophet Mohammad (S).

644 Uthman, a wealthy merchant from the rich and powerful Umayyad clan, was elected successor by a council named by Umar before his death.

Uthman continued the conquests that had steadily increased the size of the Islamic empire, but the victories now came at a greater cost and brought less booty in return.

Uthman distributed many of the provincial governorships to members of his family. Thus, much of the treasure received by the central government went to Uthman's family and to other provincial governors.

647 Mu'awiya built a Syrian tribal army strong enough to repel a Byzantine attack.

649 Mu'awiya followed a series of campaigns against the Byzantines, which resulted in the capture of Cyprus.

650 To maintain uniformity, copies of the Qur'an collected from all Muslim territory were compared and one standard version was released and redistributed.

651 Trying to seek refuge in one province after another, Yazdgerd III was at last murdered near Merv.

____ Persia officially became a Muslim state.

652 Muslim armies continued to Khorasan.

Most of the Muslim victories took place under Caliph Uthman.

____ Uthman appointed the Umayyads as governors of the occupied districts.

____ Violations of peace terms were severely punished.

____ People were forced to pay a toll tax and a land tax.

____ The inhabitants of invaded lands were incorporated into Islamic society as protected foreigners.

At the time of conquest there was no immediate obligation for conversion. Very few examples of compulsory conversion are recorded. The new religion was far simpler than the Sassanian ritualistic Zoroastrianism. The inclination was to eliminate racial inequality and discrimination and to help the poor. This was a period of radical changes in Persian society.

653 Abu Sufyan, the influential Meccan merchant, died.

____ Muslims made separate treaties with each town or district.

Tribute rather than conversion was the main immediate concern. Existing local tax structure and social order remained almost unchanged except for warriors.

654 Mu'awiya captured Rhodes in Greece.

655 Mu'awiya defeated the Byzantine navy off the coast of Lycia in Anatolia.

656 A group of rebels besieged Uthman in his home, and after several days of fighting he was killed.

Uthman's death marked the beginning of open religious and political conflicts within the Islamic community.

656 **Imam Ali (A) was invited by the Muslims of Medina to accept the Caliphate. Reluctant, he agreed only after long hesitation.**

Imam Ali (A)'s brief reign was beset by difficulties due mostly to the corrupt state of affairs he inherited.

Imam Ali (A) based his rule on the Islamic ideals of social justice and equality. His policy was a blow to the interests of the Quraysh aristocracy of Mecca who had grown rich in the wake of the Muslim conquests.

656 **The Quraysh demanded that Imam Ali (A) bring the murderers of Uthman to trial, and when he rejected their request, a rebellion against him was instigated.**

The leaders of the rebellion were Talha and Zubair, two prominent Meccans, along with A'isha, Mohammad (S)'s widow. This rebellion, known as the Battle of the Camel, was quelled. The engagement derived its name from the fierce fighting that centered around the camel upon which A'isha was mounted.

656 **Mu'awiya, a kinsman of the slain Caliph Uthman, bore the duty of revenge.**

Because Imam Ali (A) neglected to apprehend and punish Uthman's murderers, Mu'awiya regarded him as an accomplice to the murder and refused to acknowledge his Caliphate.

____ **Persians provided advisors to the Muslims.**

657 **Imam Ali (A) marched to the Euphrates border of Syria and engaged Mu'awiya's troops at the famous Battle of Siffin.**

Mu'awiya's guile turned near defeat into a truce. Resorting to a trick that played upon the religious sensibilities of Imam Ali (A)'s forces, he persuaded the enemy to enter into negotiations that ultimately cast doubt on the legitimacy of Imam Ali (A)'s Caliphate and alienated a sizable number of his supporters, who came to be known as Kharijites.

____ The Kharijites under the leadership of Ibn Wahab were opposed equally to Imam Ali (A)'s claims and to those of

658 The Battle of Nahrawan was fought between Imam Ali (A) and the Kharijites. Ibn Wahab and most of his followers were killed.

658 During the rebellion of the Kharijites, Mu'awiya took advantage of Imam Ali (A)'s difficulties in Iraq to send a force to seize control of Egypt.

658 Hormozan became a military advisor to the Muslims in Medina.

660 Muslims consolidated their rule in Persia.

661 Ali (A) was assassinated in Kufa by a Kharijite, Ibn Muljam.

661 Having held both Syria and Egypt, Mu'awiya, the commander of the largest force in Muslim Empire, had the strongest claim to the Caliphate.

Meanwhile many of the Imam Ali (A)'s followers pledged their loyalty to Imam Ali (A)'s elder son, Imam Hassan (A). They considered Imam Hassan (A) to be the rightful heir to Mohammad (S)'s position of leadership.

661 Mu'awiya refused to acknowledge Imam Hassan (A) as Caliph and began to prepare for war.

Imam Hassan (A) dispatched a force to meet Mu'awiya and then himself headed a larger force. With little money left, Imam Hassan (A), was plagued by defections from his army. Although some of his followers resented it fiercely, he opened peace negotiations and later in the year abdicated the Caliphate to Mu'awiya.

Umayyad Period

661 – 750

Umayyads, founded by Muawiyah and headed by Abu Sufyan, were a largely merchant family of the Quraysh tribe centered at Mecca. They had initially resisted Islam, not converting until 627. Umayyad was the first Arab Muslim dynasty of religious and secular caliphs to rule over the conquered nations. The caliphs ruled initially from Medina in present day Saudi Arabia, then from Damascus, Syria. Under the Umayyad dynasty, political and social ascendancy remained in the hands of a few Arab families from Mecca and Medina. This caused the Muslim population, which had grown enormously as the empire expanded, to become increasingly discontented, especially since the Umayyads had found it necessary to increase their income from taxation.

661 Mu'awiya founded the Umayyad dynasty of Caliphs and made Damascus his capital.

It is ironic that a man who became the political-religious head of Islam was born into the family of Abu Sufyan, who rejected the Prophet in his home city, Mecca, and continued to oppose him on the battlefield after he had emigrated to Medina. Mu'awiya did not become a Muslim until Mohammad (S) had conquered Mecca.

____ The Umayyads shifted the focal point of Muslim political power to Damascus.

680 Hassan Ibn Ali (A) passed away in Medina.

680 Umayyad Caliph Mu'awiya died, and his son Yazid succeeded him as the leader of all Muslim territories.

Imam Hossein (A), the third Imam of the Shias, was invited by the governor of Medina to take an oath of allegiance to Yazid.

680 Imam Hossein (A) refused to recognize the legitimacy of Yazid.

680 Imam Hossein (A) was invited by the townsmen of Kufa, a city in Iraq with a Shia majority, to go there and raise the banner of revolt against the Umayyads.

680 Imam Hossein (A) set out for Kufa with a small band of relations and followers.

He was inspired by a definite ideology to found a regime that would reinstate a true Islamic rule as opposed to what he considered the unjust rule of the Umayyads.

According to the traditional accounts, he met the poet al-Farazdaq on the way and was told that the hearts of the people of Kufa were for him, but their swords were for the Umayyads.

____ The governor of Iraq, on behalf of the Caliph, sent 4,000 men to arrest Imam Hossein (A) and his small company.

680 The Umayyads massacred Imam Hossein (A) along with his 72 comrades in arms, and took the women and children of his family captive on Ashura, the tenth day of the lunar month of Muharram.

Imam Hossein (A) was trapped at Karbala, near the banks of the Euphrates. He gave his companions the choice to leave him to his fate, but 72 of his men refused to desert him. Despite the odds, Imam Hossein (A) took the high ground of principle by declaring that death is preferable to compromise between right and wrong. The Tragedy of Karbala (Ashura) was a most perfect example of piety sacrificing itself for justice.

This battle seemingly helped secure the position of the Umayyads for a short time, but among Shia Muslims the day, even month, of Imam Hossein (A)'s Martyrdom became an annual holy time of public mourning to express solidarity with him.

691 **Dome of the Rock (Qubbat us-Sakhra) was completed on the platform formerly occupied by Solomon's Temple at Jerusalem, under the Caliph Abdul Malik.**

Primarily intended for pilgrimage, this commemorative monument with Byzantine influences in the design is widely considered as probably the first superior work of architecture of Islamic period. Its central rock evokes Arabian litholatry, association of the Creation and the Last Judgment and the Prophet Mohammad (S)'s Night Journey to Heaven.

693 Muslims defeated the Greeks.

696 **Umayyads had the Greek and Pahlavi records translated into Arabic, and discarded the originals.**

698 Muslims captured Carthage, in Tunisia.

Muslims conquered some provinces of Byzantine Empire and all of those of Sassanians. Muslims retained all of the Sassanian imperial traditions. Persian Muslims were clients of certain Muslim families and tribes throughout the empire. There was an uprising to end the influence of Muslim tribes and division among Muslims. The success of the revolution launched a series of religious movements in Khorasan.

710 Raabia al-Adawiyya was born to a very poor family near Basra.

She became promoted to the rank of Sufi Saint.

710 Muslim conquest of Africa was completed.

710 Muslims began conquest of Transoxiana. They reached India.

711 Muslims, led by general Tariq Ibn Ziyad, invaded Spain.

715 Umayyad Mosque was built in Damascus.

Having purchased the complex that had for centuries served as the Roman temple of Jupiter Damascenus and Christian church of St. John the Baptist, the Caliph al-Walid had the entire site Islamicized, and made it into a mosque. Following the revered model of the Prophet (S)'s house, he had the enclosure walls used as the walls of the mosque, had the church in the center razed, and the major facade of the building turned inside out for it to face the interior courtyard. This inward looking facade became one of the most characteristic features of Islamic architecture.

728 Ibn Sirin (b.654), renowned Muslim interpreter of dreams, died.

He was also a traditionalist, renowned for his piety and for the reliability of the information he handed on.

740 Khirbat al-Mafjar, the best-known example of Umayyad secular architecture, was built near Jericho, north of the Dead Sea.

The complex had a square palace, an enclosed court in front with fountain, a bath, a mosque, and a service building. It is a loosely planned combination of the separate units found in the Roman and Byzantine palaces.

740 Imam Ja'far Sadiq (A) ("Ja'far the Trustworthy") the sixth Imam of Shia Muslims, flourished.

He was the son of the fifth Imam, Mohammad Baqir (A) and great-grandson of Imam Ali (A).

Various Muslim writers have ascribed three fundamental religious ideas to him. First, he adopted a middle road about the question of predestination, asserting that God decreed some things absolutely but left others to human agency – a compromise that was widely adopted. Second, in the science of Hadith, he proclaimed the principle that what was contrary to the Qur'an should be rejected, whatever other evidence might support it. Third, he described Mohammad (S)'s prophetic mission as a ray of light, created before Adam and passed on from Mohammad (S) to his descendants.

746 Raabia al-Adawiyya was about thirty-six years old when God awakened her.

746 A movement was led by Bihafarid who claimed to be a prophet from the line of Zoroaster.

Many more religious uprisings and campaigns against the legitimate Caliphs occurred in Khorasan and Central Asia.

749 Zoroastrians persuaded the leader of the revolution, Abu Moslem Khorasani, to kill Bihafarid.

The leader of the Abbasid movement was Abu Moslem Khorasani of Persian origin. His intention was to form a coalition of all those who opposed the Umayyads.

750 Abu Moslem defeated the last Umayyad Caliph, Marwan Hammar, and thus the Caliphate was passed down to the Abbasids.

Abbasid Period

750 – 1040

Opposition to Syrian domination centered in Persia as the legitimists allied themselves with the Abbasids, descendants from Abbas, an uncle of the prophet Muhammad (S). The Abbasids seized the caliphate following the overthrow of Umayyads, and moved the capital of the empire eastward to a new city, Baghdad, on the Tigris. For the first century or so of their caliphate, the Abbasids acted as the leaders of Islam both religiously and politically, despite the fact that during this period their authority was rejected by some. The political fragmentation of the Abbasid caliphate led to the emergence of many local courts and centers of power, which also encouraged the development of science and philosophy as well as poetry and prose, art, and architecture. Some of the local courts that emerged in the eastern regions of the caliphate are especially associated with the rise of an Islamic Persian literature and Iranian national sentiment. Abbasid caliphate came to an end when the Mongols sacked Baghdad and killed the last caliph of the line.

750 The change of dynasty marked the eclipse of Syria and a consequent weakening of Greek influence in the growing Islamic culture. It also signaled the end of purely Arab domination.

____ The advent of the Abbasids brought about many changes.

____ Abu Moslem shifted the focus of politics and culture to Iraq.

754 Abu Moslem placed the first Abbasid Caliph as-Saffah in power.

At this stage, the Abbasid Empire stretched from Spain to the Indus.

Arabic was the language of the Qur'an, learning and the learned throughout the empire. Persian scholars had mastered the Arabic language that had replaced Pahlavi, which had remained the language of the magi alone. Persian authors translated the main sources of knowledge from Pahlavi into Arabic, and the Pahlavi originals were discarded and lost.

755 Abd ur-Rahman, a member of the Umayyad ruling family of Syria, attacked and defeated the Governor of al-Andalus in Spain.

He then founded an Umayyad dynasty in Spain, Emirate of Cordoba, and made Cordoba his capital.

756 Abdollah Ibn Muqaffa (b.720), Arabic author and translator of Persian origin, died.

He was one of the first to translate literary works of the Indian and Persian civilizations into Arabic, and one of the creators of Arabic literary prose. He made a remarkable Arabic prose from the Pahlavi 'Kalileh va Demneh'. He also translated the Pahlavi 'Khodaynameh' of Dehghan Daneshvar into Arabic.

759 Abu Moslem, leader of the revolutionary Abbasid movement, was executed by order of al-Mansur, second Abbasid Caliph.

Soon after the execution of Abu Moslem, the number of uprisings increased.

762 The Abbasid Caliph al-Mansur founded Baghdad, the capital of Islamic state.

He established the new city near the former Sassanian capital of Ctesiphon on the middle course of the Tigris and Euphrates. The site had both the obvious commercial advantage of easy communication with the Persian Gulf and the Mediterranean, and the symbolic associations of succession to the ancient capital of Persia.

Like earlier Persian cities, Baghdad was round. Two sets of mud-brick walls and four gates protected it. Inside, there was a ring of residences and government bureaus with the Caliph's palace and the congregational mosque in the center.

____ In general, Abbasid culture owed a good deal to Persian culture and ceremony, and the role of late antique Mediterranean culture, apart from natural sciences, diminished.

____ Semi-independent dynasties began to establish themselves in Persia.

They acknowledged allegiance to the supreme power in Baghdad. At first, their rule gained Caliphal seal of approval as governors over their lands. Gradually, they set themselves up in opposition to the Abbasids.

765 Imam Ja'far Sadiq (A), the sixth Imam of Shia Muslims, passed away in Medina.

Divisions in Shi'ism date mainly from his death. His eldest son Ismail, predeceased him, but the 'Seveners', represented today chiefly by Ismailis (followers of Ismail), agreed that Ismail merely disappeared and would reappear one day. Three other sons also claimed the Imamate; of these, Imam Musa Kazim (A) gained the widest recognition. Shia sects following Imam Musa Kazim (A) are mostly known as "Twelvers"; they trace the succession from Ja'far to the 12th Imam.

765 Ali Ibn Musa ar-Reza (A), the eighth Imam of Shias, was born.

777 Ibrahim Adham (b.730), prominent Sufi of Balkh, died. Legends about his life spread to Persia, India and Indonesia.

777 Al-Moqanna, a native of Merv, threw the country into confusion with his claim to be an incarnation of God. He died three years later.

786 Al-Ma'mun was born six months before his half brother al-Amin.

Al-Amin was the son of a mother of Arab blood; this would give him more legitimacy in the future question of succession.

793 Sibeveyh, celebrated Persian grammarian of the Arabic language, died in Shiraz.

His monumental work is al-Kitab fi an-nahw ("The Book on Grammar"), or more simply al-Kitab ("The Book"). This large work on Arabic grammar has remained the basis of all native studies on the subject.

794 Raabia al-Adawiyya traveled to Jerusalem and lived on top of the holy Mountain of Olive. She caused an outcry among the Ulama when she announced: 'I have ceased to exist and have passed out of self. I exist in God and am altogether His'.

____ After a long hesitation, Harun ar-Rashid finally decided in favor of al-Amin as his successor to the Caliphate.

801 Raabia al-Adawiyya, famous mystic and saint of Basra, died.

The introduction of the element of love, which changed asceticism into mysticism, is ascribed to her.

802 On the occasion of a pilgrimage to Mecca, Harun ar-Rashid formally announced the respective rights of his two sons.

Al-Ma'mun recognized al-Amin as successor to the Caliphate in Baghdad, but al-Amin acknowledged his brother's sovereignty over the eastern provinces of the Empire, with his seat at Merv in Khorasan, now in Turkmenistan.

809 Harun ar-Rashid, the Abbasid Caliph, died.

His death created discord that soon developed into armed conflict between the two brothers. Al-Ma'mun was in effect stripped by al-Amin of his rights to the succession.

____ Al-Ma'mun, with the help of two Persians, managed to re-organize his power in Khorasan.

His two Persian supporters were Fazl Ibn Sahl, who was to become his vizier, and general Tahir, who founded the Tahirid dynasty in 821.

____ Tahir's victory over al-Amin on the outskirts of Reyy allowed al-Ma'mun troops to occupy western Persia.

____ Al-Amin appealed in vain to new troops recruited in part from the Arabs of Syria.

812 Al-Amin was besieged in Baghdad.

812 Bayazid Bastami, known as an exponent of intoxicated Sufism, was born.

813 Imam Reza (A), then living in Medina, was recognized among 'Ithna Ashari' ("Twelver") Shias as the eighth Imam.

813 After desperate resistance, Baghdad was taken by al-Ma'mun's forces.

Al-Amin who had in the meantime been declared deposed as Caliph in Iraq and Arabia, wished to surrender but was killed — contrary, it seems to al-Ma'mun's orders. Thus ended one of the most devastating civil wars known to the Islamic East.

____ Al-Ma'mun, having become Caliph of the entire Abbasid Empire and assisted by his faithful Persian vizier Fazl, decided to continue to reside at Merv.

815 Jabir Ibn Hayyan (b.ca.721), the great alchemist, died in Kufa.

He revised the ancient belief that everything was composed of fire, earth, water, and air. He believed that these four elements combined to form mercury and sulphur and that all metals are formed from these two substances. More than 2,000 works are attributed to him.

816 Babak Khorramdin, the leader of Persian Khorramdins, allied himself north of Ardabil with the neighboring Armenians and obtained support from the Emperor Theophilus.

Khorramdins were followers of a religious sect that emerged after the execution of Abu Moslem in 759. Denying that Abu Moslem was dead, the sect predicted that he would return to spread justice throughout the world.

____ Babak Khorramdin revolted in Azerbaijan threatening communications between the Caliphate and the eastern Caucasus and causing the Caliphate great losses in men and money.

817 Al-Ma'mun designated as his heir not a member of his own family but instead Imam Reza (A) known for his piety and learning.

This was an attempt to heal the division between the majority Sunnis and the Shias. Al-Ma'mun gave Imam Reza (A) his own daughter as a wife. As a further symbol of reconciliation, he adopted the green flag in place of the traditional black flag of the Abbasid family.

____ The appointment aroused varying reactions.

The Sunnis of Iraq, already irritated by al-Ma'mun's transfer of the capital from Baghdad to Merv and exasperated by his ill deeds, rose up in rebellion.

____ The people of Baghdad deposed al-Ma'mun and proclaimed as the new Caliph the Abbasid Prince Ibrahim, son of the third Caliph al-Mahdi (r.775-785).

818 When the new wave of insurrection in Baghdad finally reached al-Ma'mun, he abruptly decided to leave Merv for Baghdad.

818 During the long journey from Merv to Baghdad, two dramatic events took place; the vizier Fazl was assassinated and Imam Reza (A) passed away at Tus.

Shia historians ascribed Imam Reza (A)'s death to poisoning, administered by al-Ma'mun. His shrine in Mashad became a very important pilgrimage center for the Shias.

821 Tahir Ibn Hossein, the former general of al-Ma'mun, founded the Tahirid dynasty in Khorasan.

822 Tahir died a few days after he omitted the name of al-Ma'mun from the Friday Sermon, the Khutba.

____ Al-Ma'mun elected Tahir's son, Abdollah, as his successor.

828 Abdollah Ibn Tahir, with his exceptional administrative gifts, managed to consolidate the dynasty's power.

____ In the west, the Tahirids occupied Reyy for some time and extended their power to the Caspian provinces, where they met resistance from the Alavids established in Dailam.

837 Babak Khorramdin led a new revolt against the Abbasids that was put down.

838 Babak Khorramdin died.

840 Muslims made conquests in Southern Italy.

842 Muslims captured Bari in South Italy and made it their base.

844 Abdollah Ibn Tahir, member of the Tahirid dynasty, died. He was a poet, general and virtually independent ruler of Khorasan, a man of wisdom and an accomplished musician.

846 Muslims laid Rome under siege.

By mid-ninth century, Abbasid political unity was about to crumble.

850 Al-Kharazmi (b.780 in Baghdad), mathematician, astronomer and geographer, died.

His work on mathematics, 'Kitab al-jabr wa al-muqabalah' ("The Book of Integration and Equation"), was translated into Latin in the 12th century whereof the term algebra originated. A science completely unknown was thus introduced into Europe. Another work on Hindu-Arabic numerals is preserved only in a Latin translation, 'Algoritmi de numero Indorum' ("Al-Kharazmi concerning the Hindu Art of Reckoning"). From the title originated the term algorithm.

852 The mosque of al-Mutawakkil was built in Samarra.

This mosque with an area of about 3.7 hectares, nearly two and a half times the size of the Umayyad mosque in Damascus, remained for centuries the largest mosque in the world. It's most innovative architectural feature is its spiral tower, one of the earliest existing minarets. This minaret, originally more than 50 m (170 ft) tall, stands outside the mosque proper opposite the mihrab. Around the outside of the tower, there is a ramp of increasing slope that winds from the base to the summit, on which there was once a pavilion.

858 Ya'qub Leis took part in a revolt against the Tahirid governor.

860 Alamut Fortress was made by a ruler of Dailam.

861 Ya'qub Leis Saffari was proclaimed Lord of Sistan.

865 Zakariya Razi, a celebrated alchemist and Muslim philosopher, was born in Reyy.

867 The Saffarids, who were in origin and policy the antithesis of the Tahirids, came to power under the command of Ya'qub Leis.

____ Ya'qub occupied Herat and Pushang.

____ In a peace treaty with the Tahirids, the authority of Ya'qub Leis over the whole of southern Persia, including Kerman and Fars, was recognized.

____ Persian, a version of spoken Pahlavi and Arabic, had become the official language of semi-independent principalities.

____ Revival of Sassanian glories had become a symbol of Persian patriotism.

____ A tendency had developed to use Persian as a reaction to all that was Arab and Arabic.

____ Ya'qub appointed Abdorrazzaq to translate Khodaynameh from Pahlavi into Persian and had it updated by noble descendants of Sassanians. This he called 'Shahnameh' ("The Book of Kings").

The resurgence of Persia and Persian poetry began from the time of Saffarids, who forced their secretaries to write in Persian.

870 Ya'qub Leis waged war against Ghazna, Kabul and Balkh.

870 Mohammad Ibn Ismail al-Bukhari (b.810), famous traditionalist, died. He is known for his collection of Prophetic traditions, called 'al-Sahih'.

870 Abu Yusuf Ya'qub al-Kindi, the first outstanding Islamic philosopher, known as 'the philosopher of the Arabs', died.
He concerned himself not only with those philosophical questions that had been treated by the Aristotelian Neoplatonists of Alexandria but also with such miscellaneous subjects as astrology, medicine, Indian arithmetic, logogriphs, the manufacture of swords, and cooking. He is known to have written more than 270 works (mostly short treatises), a considerable number of which are extant, some in Latin translations.

873 Ya'qub Leis marched against the Tahirid sovereign.

874 Bayazid (Abu Yazid) Bastami, one of the most celebrated Islamic mystics, died.
Some five hundred of his sayings have been handed down.

876 Ya'qub Leis led his troops to Baghdad.

____ Having been deserted by some of his officers, Ya'qub was forced to withdraw to Khuzestan.

878 Muslims took Syracuse and almost completed conquest of Sicily.

878 Imam Mohammad al-Mahdi (A), the twelfth and the last Imam of twelver Shias, disappeared.
It is believed that he has been concealed by God, and that he will reappear in time as the messianic deliverer. This doctrine is known as Ghaiba or occultation.

879 Having fought a series of battles for independence, Ya'qub Leis Saffari died.
His attempts ended in failure, but his gesture provided the first warning that the Caliphate's authority was threatened.

____ Ya'qub was succeeded by his no less famous brother, Amr, who took over the titles and also the position of honorary governor of Baghdad.

880 Tari Kahaneh mosque in Damghan was constructed.
This simple mosque, described as one of the most magnificent buildings in Islam, is the oldest existing Islamic structure recorded in Persia. Apart from its slightly pointed arches, this building is purely Sassanian in terms of material, structure, and technique. It has the typically square inner-court surrounded by arcades of tunnel vaults set on huge round piers 3.5 m (12 ft) high and almost 2 m (7 ft) in diameter.

884 Hamdun al-Qassar, founder of the Malamatiyyeh mystical order, died.
According to Malamatiyyeh, all outward appearance of piety, including good deeds, was ostentation.

892 The first great Samanid sovereign, Ismail Ibn Ahmad, conquered Khorasan in a victory over the Saffarid Amr, who was later taken prisoner.
Samanids came from the village of Saman in the province of Balkh.

893 End of 72 years of Tahirid rule.
During their reign, Tahirid rulers remained faithful to the Caliphs and showed no sign of nationalistic aims.

____ In the Islamic world a series of dynasties and principalities emerged.
The Abbasid Empire began to fall apart, with its authority ultimately divided and limited to Iraq.

902 Ismail Samani led his troops to Zanjan.

____ Amr was murdered in the prison of Ismail Samani.

903 Ismail Samani died.

906 The first Frankish embassy to Baghdad was set up.

909 Fatimid Caliphate was founded in North Africa.
Fatimids tried unsuccessfully to overthrow the Abbasid Caliphs as leaders of the Islamic world.

911 Samanid troops occupied Sistan.
Under the Samanids, Bukhara and Samarqand, two of the main trade centers of the Silk Route, became the melting pot from which modern Persian language was produced. It was to acquire the dignity of being the cultural and administrative language of the region.

912 Abd ur-Rahman III, the greatest Umayyad ruler of Cordoba, succeeded his grand father as the Emir of Cordoba at 21.

912 Ibn Rusta, historian and geographer from Isfahan, died.
The one volume which is left of what must have been a very voluminous work, may be defined as a short encyclopedia of historical and geographical knowledge.

920 Dailam warriors occupied central Persia and cut communication lines between Khorasan and Baghdad.

922 Abul Mughith Hallaj (b.857 at Tur), Arabic-speaking mystic theologian, was executed in Baghdad for having proclaimed 'I am (God) the Truth'.
The drama of his life and death became a reference point in Islamic history for adherence to mysticism.

923 Abu Ja'far Mohammad Ibn Jarir Tabari (b.ca.839 in Amol), Muslim scholar, died in Baghdad.
He was the author of enormous compendiums of early Islamic history and Qur'anic interpretations, and made a distinct contribution to the consolidation of Sunni thought during the 9th century. He laid the foundations for both Qur'anic and historical sciences. His major works were the 'Qur'an Commentary' and the 'Tarikh ar-Rusul wa al-Muluk' ("History of Prophets and Kings"). The latter is in fact a history of the world up to the year 915. It is known in the West as 'Annals'.

925 Zakariyya Razi (Rhazes), the greatest physician of the Islamic world and the discoverer of alcohol, died in Reyy.
Razi's two most significant medical works are the 'Kitab al-Mansuri', which he composed for the Reyy ruler Mansur Ibn Is'haq and which became well known in the West in Gerard

of Cremona's 12th-century Latin translation; and 'Kitab al-Hawi' ("Comprehensive Book"), in which he surveyed Greek, Syrian, and early Arabic medicine, as well as some Indian medical knowledge. Throughout his works, he added his own considered judgment and medical experience as commentary.

928 **Mardavij Ibn Ziyar united and ruled a substantial part of southern and central Persia under the new dynasty of Ziyarids.**

____ **Three Persian brothers from Dailam in the Caspian region began their careers as soldiers in the service of Mardavij.**
The three brothers later founded the Buyid dynasty ruling the Persian plateau. Ali, the eldest brother, consolidated power in Isfahan and Fars, Hassan occupied Reyy and Hamadan, and Ahmad took Kerman.

929 Abd ur-Rahman III (d.961), took the title of the first Caliph of the Umayyad Arab Muslim dynasty of Spain.
Thus Emirate of Cordoba became Caliphate. There now existed three Caliphates.

934 **Mardavij seized Isfahan, Azerbaijan and Hamadan.**

935 **Mardavij was assassinated by one of his Turkish guards, and his brother, Vushmgir (the quail catcher), succeeded him.**

935 **Abul Hassan Ash'ari (b.873), theologian and founder of the Ash'ariyyeh, died.**
He left the Mu'tazila for the orthodox traditionalists, the Sunnis, but defended his new beliefs by the type of argument employed by the Mu'tazila.

940 **Ferdowsi, who became one of the greatest Persian poets and the author of the epic of Shahnameh, was born to a wealthy family of Dehqans.**

940 **Ibn Muqla (b.885), vizier of the Abbasid court and a famous calligrapher, died.**

940 **Al-Kulaini, Imami transmitter of traditions, died.**

His work , known as 'al-Kafi' is mostly a collection of traditions of the Imams. It became to be considered one of the most authoritative collections of traditions on which Imami jurisprudence is based.

940 **Abu Abdollah Ja'far Rudaki (b.859 at Rudak, Khorasan), one of the great Persian poets, died.**

Widely regarded as the father of Persian poetry, he was the first poet of note to compose poems in the 'New Persian', written in Arabic alphabet. Approximately 100,000 couplets are attributed to Rudaki, but of that enormous output, fewer than 1,000 have survived, and these are scattered among many anthologies and biographical works. One of his most important contributions to literature is his translation of 'Kalila va Dimna' from Arabic into New Persian.

'Kalila va Dimna' was a collection of fables of Indian origin. Later retellings of these fables owe much to this lost translation of Rudaki, which further ensured his fame in Perso-Islamic literature.

943 **Ibn Hawqal, Arab geographer of Nisibis in Upper Mesopotamia, began his series of journeys.**

He was one of the best exponents of geography based on travel and direct observation. His main work is called 'Configuration of the Earth'.

943 **Abul Hassan Nasafi, distinguished philosopher-theologian of the Ismailis in Khorasan and Transoxiana, died.**

He was generally credited with the introduction of Neo-Platonic philosophy into Ismaili circles.

943 **Vushmgir, established in Reyy, was deposed by the Dailamites.**

943 **The domed square mausoleum was brought to a pitch of perfection in the so-called "Tomb of the Samanids" in Bukhara.**

This fire temple in Islamic dress is a precocious masterpiece in brick, integrating compact monumentality with refined all-over geometric ornament. This is the earliest dynastic mausoleum to survive anywhere in the Islamic lands.

946 **One of the three brothers, Ahmad Ibn Buya , entered Baghdad and swore an oath of loyalty to the Caliph.**

The formation of the Buyid sovereignty remained a memorable event in the history of Persia, as the whole country was under the rule of Persian princes. Buyids, like the rest of the population of Dailam, were firm supporters of the Shias.

947 **Basra was captured, adding to the third side of a triangle administrated by Dailamites, whose territory extended to Reyy, Shiraz and Baghdad.**

Each of these three cities was governed by one of the three brothers, whose ties of blood kept them loyal to each other. Besides exercising extensive political power, the Shia Dailamite princes were patrons of learning.

950 **Abu Nasr Farabi (b.878 in Turkestan), also called Alfarabius, Alpharabius or Avennasar, one of the most outstanding and renowned Muslim philosophers, died, probably in Damascus.**

He was known as 'the second teacher', the first being Aristotle. He was influenced by the Aristotelian teaching in Baghdad and the late Alexandrian interpretation of Greek philosophy. Avicenna and Averroes appreciated him highly.

951 **The earliest of the single barrel-vaulted ivan-mosques still surviving, was repaired and added to at Neiriz.**

960 **Jame' mosque of Na'in was constructed.**

This is one of the most ancient mosques built on Abbasid design that clearly demonstrates the old Persian urge for verticality as opposed to the horizontality that had dominated the Tari Khaneh or the solidity of Ismail's tomb. This urge reappeared at Na'in in sharply pointed tunnel vaults, which are nearly three times as high as they are wide. This mosque is still in regular use.

961 **Hamzeh Isfahani, Persian philologist and historian, died.**

He is the author of a well-known chronology of pre-Islamic and Islamic dynasties.

967 Abul Faraj Isfahani (b.897), author of the well-known Book of Songs, died.

The book is a collection of songs chosen by famous musicians, to which Abul Faraj added rich information about the poets who were the authors of the songs, and about ancient Arab tribes.

967 Abu Sa'id Abul Khair was born.

Bal'ami, minister of Mansur Samani, appointed Daqiqi to set Shahnameh into verse.

Daqiqi was the chief poet of the court of Mansur Samani.

973 Abureihan Biruni, who became one of the most original and profound Muslim scholars, was born in Khwarezm, Khorasan.

976 Qabus Ibn Vushmgir continued the rule of the Ziyarids.

Qabus Ibn Vushmgir was known for his literary abilities and his patronage of the great scholars of his time.

Biruni dedicated his first works to Qabus Ibn Vushmgir.

977 Sebuktigin founded the Ghaznavid dynasty.

He was a former Turkish slave who was recognized by the Samanids (a Persian Muslim dynasty) as governor of Ghazna, now in Afghanistan. As the Samanid dynasty weakened, Sebuktigin consolidated his position and expanded his domains as far as the Indian border.

980 Abu Mansur Mohammad Daqiqi (b.930) died.

He composed the 1,058 couplets which form the oldest-known text of the 'Book of Kings', the national epic of Persia.

980 Ferdowsi began to create his lifetime masterpiece.

He used some 1,000 of the 1,058 couplets of Daqiqi in the preface of his own Shahnameh.

980 Avicenna (Ibn Sina), who became one of the greatest Persian scientists and philosophers, was born in Fergana near Bukhara.

986 Abd ur-Rahman Ibn Umar as-Sufi (b.903) died.
He was an eminent astronomer at the court of the Dailamites. His best-known work is a description of the fixed stars.

991 Abu Ja'far Mohammad Ibn Babawayh (b.923), a prolific author and one of the foremost doctors and traditionalists of Shias, died.

997 Mahmud of Ghazna ascended the Ghaznavid throne.
He continued the expansionist policy of his father.

____ Mahmud of Ghazna heard of and praised Ferdowsi's work of Rostam and Esfandiyar, the prime figures of the Shahnameh.
Mahmud summoned Abol Qasim Mansur to his court and gave him the title of 'Ferdowsi', meaning one who made the court of the Sultan a paradise.

1004 Nasir Khosrow, who became a great Persian poet, prose writer, noted traveler and Ismaili philosopher and missionary, was born at Qobadian near Merv in Khorasan.

1005 The Samanid territories were divided. The river Oxus formed the boundary between the two successor states to the Samanid Empire, the Ghaznavids ruling in the west and the Qarakhanids in the east.

1006 The tomb tower perhaps reached its climax of perfection in the Gonbad-e Qabus.
Dominating the surrounding countryside, this magnificent 51 m (170 ft) fired brick cylindrical tower crowns an artificial mound. The monument has ten knife-edge flanges girdling the central cylinder in a remarkably modern design.

1010 Ferdowsi completed his masterpiece of Shahnameh.
The 'Book of Kings', a poem of 60,000 couplets, brought together the history of Persia from mythical times down to the overthrow of the Sassanians by the Muslims. The exploits of heroes, among them the famous Rostam, are interwoven with love stories.

In the composition of the Shahnameh, Ferdowsi tried to refrain from using any Arabic words, which led to the revival of pre-Islamic Persian culture.

____ Avicenna went to the Ziyarid court of Qabus Ibn Vushmgir.

1012 Qabus Ibn Vushmgir was deposed by his courtiers and his son, Manuchehr.

Manuchehr later submitted himself to Mahmud of Ghazna, and married his daughter.

1015 Seyyed Razi, the celebrated Islamic theologian, died.

He collected Imam Ali's political discourses, sermons, letters, and sayings in a book entitled Nahj ul-Balagha ("Road of Eloquence").

1016 Toghril, the grandson of Saljuq, chief of the Oghuz tribes in the Jand region, with his brother Chaghri entered Muslim Transoxiana. Toghril was to found Saljuq dynasty in 1038.

During the 10th-century migrations of the Turkish peoples from Central Asia and southeast Russia, one group of nomadic tribes led by their chief, Saljuq, had settled in the lower reaches of the Jaxartes river and later converted to the Sunni form of Islam. They played a part in the frontier defense forces of the Samanids and later of Mahmud of Ghazna.

1018 Nezam ol-Molk, who became a great organizer of the Saljuq Empire, was born at Tus.

1021 Ferdowsi died in poverty.

Ferdowsi became the founder of the romantic narrative poem which was to have a brilliant future in Persia. He had a profound and lasting influence on Persian literature and on the spirit of the people of Persia.

1021 Mausoleum of Pir-e Alamdar, the earliest dated round tomb tower in Persia, was constructed.

1022 Ibn al-Bawwab, famous calligrapher of the Dailamite period, died.

He perfected the style of writing invented by the vizier Ibn Muqla.

1025 Toghril, Chaghri and their uncle Arsalan entered the service of the Turkish Qarakhanid prince of Bukhara.

1025 Defeated by Mahmud of Ghazna, Toghril and Chaghri took refuge in Khwarezm (around the estuary of the Jaxartes river southeast of the Aral Sea), while Arsalan settled in Khorasan.

1026 The minaret of Tari Khaneh mosque in Damghan was built on the order of the chamberlain Abu Harb Bakhtiar.

This now 26 m (85 ft) lofty cylindrical Saljuq type minaret, which probably had an upper gallery for the muezzin, is one of the earliest minarets set on a polygonal plinth and decorated with inscription bands and geometric brick patterns.

____ After their kinsmen in Khorasan had been driven by Mahmud to western Persia, Toghril and Chaghri entered Khorasan, where, having established close ties with the orthodox Muslim groups in the large towns, they subdued Merv and Nishapur.

1029 Sultan Mahmud removed the Dailamites of Reyy from Throne.

1030 Sultan Mahmud of Ghazna died, and his son Mas'ud became Sultan.

Ghaznavid power reached its zenith during Mahmud's reign. He created an empire that stretched from the Oxus to the Indus Valley and the Indian Ocean; in the west he captured (from the Buyids) the Persian cities of Reyy and Hamadan. A devout Muslim, Mahmud reshaped the Ghaznavids from their non-Muslim Turkic origins into an Islamic dynasty and expanded the frontiers of Islam.

1030 Meskavayh, Persian philosopher and historian from Reyy, died.

As a philosopher, he is distinguished by the central importance he attached to ethics. His universal history spans from the Flood to the year 980, but only the last part, dealing with the Dailamites, is original.

1033 Sheikh Abu Is'haq Kazeruni (b.963), founder of a Sufi order variously known as Morshediyyeh, Eshraqiyyeh and Kazeruniyyeh, died.

He is known for his charitable concern for the poor, which trend was followed by all the branches of the order.

1036 The Davazdah Imam (12 Imams) mausoleum was built in Yazd.

This simple but powerful domed building is a plain, solid brick structure with deep squinches that merge upward and outward to reach and carry the ring of the dome. The interior of the squinches is composed of three arched panels, consisting of a half-dome flanked and supported by two lower and shallow quarter-dome panels. This architectural form reached its perfection in Saljuq architecture.

1037 Avicenna (Ibn Sina), primarily known as a philosopher and physician, died at 57 in Hamadan.

He contributed to all sciences accessible in his day. 131 authentic and 110 doubtful works are listed in his bibliography. Among his most famous works are the 'Book of Healing', a vast philosophical and scientific encyclopedia; the 'Canon of Medicine', one of the most famous books in the history of medicine; and the 'Tale of Hayy Ibn Yaqzan', a philosophical allegory. Avicenna's influence on medieval European philosophers such as Michael Scot, Alberta Magnus, Roger Bacon, Duns Scouts and Thomas Aquinas is undeniable.

1037 Abul Hassan Farrokhi-Sistani, celebrated Persian poet, died.

He was attached to the court of Mahmud Ibn Sebuktigin of Ghazna, singing his poems to his own accompaniment on the lute. The collected edition of his poems contains more than 9,500 lines of verse.

Saljuq Period

1040 – 1256

Saljuqs, originally a clan belonging to the Oghuz, a Turkmen tribe of Central Asia, converted to Sunni Islam in the 10th century, and began migrating to Iran in the 11th century. They conquered most of Iran and Baghdad, but this made no significant difference to the position of the Abbasid caliphs as the Saljuqs made themselves protectors of the caliph of Baghdad. Only in times of Saljuq weakness were individual caliphs occasionally able to exercise some power and influence. Ruling from their capital at Isfahan in Iran, the Saljuq rulers who were given the title sultan by the caliph used the Persian language in their administration and were patrons of Persian literature. The Saljuqs encouraged a renaissance in architecture, founded numerous monuments and colleges to train future administrators in accordance with Sunni doctrine, and made war on the Shia Muslims, who rejected the caliph's authority. The main enemy of the Saljuqs was the Shia Fatimid dynasty of Egypt.

1040 The Saljuqs inflicted a decisive defeat on Sultan Mas'ud at Dandanqan. Mas'ud lost control of Khorasan, his main holding in Persia. Khorasan was then formed into a principality for Chaghri, while Toghril was left free to conquer the Persian plateau.
Mas'ud withdrew to Lahore in his Indian domains, from where his successors ruled until overtaken by the Ghurids in 1186.

1041 Abol Najm Manuchehri, the third and last of the major panegyrists of the early Ghaznavid court, died.
He was third after Onsori and Farrokhi Sistani, the chief poets of the Ghaznavid court. Unlike his contemporary Persian-writing poets, he was enthusiastic for Arabic poetry and his engaging lyricism is remarked upon by all commentators.

1044 Having already occupied the Caspian areas of Khorasan, Reyy, and Hamadan, Toghril established his suzerainty over Isfahan.
The first Saljuq conquests were generally made by the Turkmen raiders led by Toghril's foster brother Ibrahim Inal. He himself then followed to administer the conquered territories.

1048 Omar Khayyam, a highly revered Persian scientist and poet, was born in Nishapur.

1048 Ibn Zaila, pupil of Avicenna, mathematician and excellent musician, died.

1049 Toghril sent expeditions of Turkmens into the Byzantine lands of Anatolia

1049 Abu Sa'id Abol Kheir (b.967) died.
He was a Persian mystic, known for his extreme ascetic practices and his service to the poor.

1049 Abol Qasim Hassan Onsori, Persian poet, died.
He owes his fame to a collection of poetry, which contains love-poems and panegyrics. Among the latter, many are written in praise of the Ghaznavid Mahmud Ibn Sebuktigin.

1050 Biruni died in Ghazna, now in Afghanistan.

He was an outstanding mathematician , astronomer, physicist, geographer, historian, chronologist, and linguist, and an impartial observer of customs and creeds. Biruni's most famous works are 'Athar ul-baqiya' ("Chronology of Ancient Nations"); 'at-Tafhim' ("Elements of Astrology"); 'al-Qanun al-Mas'udi' ("The Mas'udi Canon"), a major work on astronomy, which he dedicated to Sultan Mas'ud of Ghazna; 'Ta'rikh al-Hind' ("A History of India"); and 'Kitab as-Saydalah' ("A treatise on drugs used in medicine"). In his works on astronomy, he discussed with approval the theory of the Earth's rotation on its axis and made accurate calculations of latitude and longitude. In his discussions on physics, he explained natural springs by the laws of hydrostatics and determined with remarkable accuracy the specific weight of 18 precious stones and metals.

1054 Toghril sent another series of Turkmen expeditions into Anatolia.

This was an attempt to prevent Turkmen raids into the surrounding Muslim territories while at the same time increasing Saljuq power against the Byzantine Empire.

1055 Fakhreddin As'ad Gorgani, author of the first-known courtly romance in Persian, called 'Veis and Ramin', died.

1055 After conquering the principalities to the east and north of Iraq, Toghril entered Baghdad, where he was commissioned to overthrow the Shia Fatimid Caliphs of Cairo in Egypt and to restore, under the Abbasid Caliph, the religious and political unity of the Islamic world.

1056 Gonbad-e Ali, the earliest dated octagonal tomb tower in Persia, was built at Abarkuh.

____ Prince Inal with his Turkmens revolted in Mesopotamia and Persia.

Discontent among Toghril's supporters over administration and reward for services resulted in a general uprising against him.

1058 A coalition of Arab and Shia Buyid forces, financed and controlled by the Fatimids of Cairo and led by Basasiri, entered Baghdad.

The Abbasid Caliph al-Qa'im was imprisoned, and prayers were recited in the name of the Fatimid Caliph of Cairo.

1060 Toghril crushed the Basasiri rebellion, regained Baghdad for the Caliph, and pacified the Arabs of Mesopotamia.

1061 Chaghri, Toghril's brother and the Saljuq ruler of Khorasan, died.

____ Toghril fought the petty princes in northwest Persia.

1062 Toghril forced the Caliph to give him a daughter in marriage in order to consolidate his high position before the Caliph.

1063 Toghril died and Alp Arsalan came to power.

Alp Arsalan was the son of Chaghri Beg and the nephew of Toghril. Alp Arsalan was sole heir to all the possessions of the dynasty except Kerman, which was held by one of his brothers, whom he promptly reduced to servitude.

____ Alp Arsalan left the administration to his wise vizier, Nezam ol-Molk, and focused on the expansion of the Saljuq realm.

____ Alp Arsalan planned his political activity in Central Asia.

He maintained peace with the Ghaznavid rulers, who were hard to track down in their mountain strongholds in India. However, he used force against the Qarakhanids of Transoxiana.

____ Alp Arsalan conducted a series of campaigns against the Byzantines and their Armenian and Georgian neighbors.

He was strongly supported by the Turkmens, who were interested in the success of the holy war against the infidels and in raids on Christian territory.

1064 Alp Arsalan seized Ani, the former Armenian capital, and Kars. These operations upset the Byzantine defense system and paved the way for the subsequent Turkish conquest of Asia Minor. They resulted in Byzantine reactions in Syria and Armenia, after which the two empires began to negotiate.

____ The Fatimid regime of Egypt and Syria began to fragment.

____ **The Ismaili community in Persia began to dig in, securing strongholds to defend their villages and land.**

The valley of the River Alamut, with its chain of impregnable fortresses dominating the trade route, soon gained an international reputation as the 'Valley of the Assassins'.

1067 **The first tomb tower at Kharaqan was completed.**

1068 **The oldest surviving Persian Dictionary, Farhang, was compiled.**

____ **Byzantine emperor Romanus IV Diogenes, with a formidable army, began assaulting Alp Arsalan's rear army in Armenia.**

The news reached Alp Arsalan when he was about to attack Aleppo, whose prince was too late in siding with the Abbasids against the Fatimids.

1071 **Alp Arsalan heavily defeated the Byzantine Emperor Romanus IV at Manzikert, now in Turkey.**

The Byzantine army, powerful in numbers but weak in morale, fell before the outnumbered but dedicated Saljuqs. By evening the Byzantine army was defeated, and, for the first time in history, a Byzantine emperor had become the prisoner of a Muslim sovereign. Alp Arsalan's goal was not to destroy the Byzantine Empire: he was content with the rectification of boundaries, the promise of tribute, and an alliance.

____ The Battle of Manzikert opened Asia Minor to Turkmen conquest. Later, every princely family in Asia Minor was to claim an ancestor who had fought on that prestigious day.

1072 **Alp Arsalan died and was buried in the Mausoleum of his father's in Merv. The new Islamic Empire was to reach its greatest splendor under his son Malik Shah.**

Alp Arsalan, who had returned to the Qarakhanid frontier, was mortally wounded during a quarrel with a prisoner. He had designated as his heir his 13-year-old son Malik Shah under the guardianship of Nezam ol-Molk.

____ Malik Shah overcame a revolt of his uncle, Qavurd (Kavurd), and an attack of the Qarakhanids of Bukhara in Khorasan

1075 A group of astronomers including Omar Khayyam devised a reformation of the calendar by the order of Malik Shah.
This calendar, which has remained the official calendar of Persia ever since, was named Jalali after Malik Shah's regal title of 'Jalal od-Dowleh'. Jalali calendar is more accurate than that of Pope Gregory, some five hundred years earlier.

1075 Nasir Khosrow died.
His travel account relates his journeys to Mecca by way of Nishapur, Tabriz, Aleppo and Jerusalem. From Mecca, he went to Cairo where he became familiar with the tradition of Ismaili learning. His Ismaili writings are the only contributions in Persian by a major Fatimid missionary. His philosophical poetry includes the 'Rowshana'inameh' ("Book of Lights"). Nasir's most celebrated prose work is the 'Safarnameh' ("Diary of a Journey Through Syria and Palestine"), describing his seven-year journey.

1076 Hassan Sabbah, the head of the Ismaili movement in Persia, went to Egypt, probably for further religious training.
He stayed there for three years, first in Cairo and then in Alexandria before he was exiled to north Africa by the Fatimid Caliph.

1077 Anustegin Gharachai was appointed governor of Khwarezm on the Oxus river by Malik Shah, and founded the Khwarezm Shah's dynasty governing the area on behalf of the Saljuqs.

1077 Abolfazl Mohammad Beihaqi (b.995), famous Persian historian, died.
He is the author of a voluminous history of the Ghaznavid dynasty.

1078 Saljuqs took almost all of Syria save the narrow coastal strip, which remained in Fatimid hands.

1079 Hassan Sabbah returned to Persia from Egypt and traveled widely in an effort to further Ismaili interests. He made a number of converts

1080 Nezam ol-Molk domed chamber in the Jame' mosque of Isfahan was built.

It was first intended as a giant maqsura for the sultan and his court, and later became the mihrab chamber of the mosque.

1081 Hassan Sabbah returned to Isfahan, briefly stopping in cities in Khuzestan trying to form new pockets of Ismailis.

During the next nine years he advocated the faith , first in Kerman and Yazd and then in Damghan.

1082 Qabus Ibn Vushmgir's grandson, who bore the same name, wrote the famous 'Mirror for Princes' or Qabusnameh.

1084 Malik Shah conquered Anatolia, and appointed Suleiman as ruler which resulted in the formation of a new local Saljuq dynasty (Saljuqs of Anatolia).

1086 The second tomb tower in open country at Kharaqan was completed.

Built most probably by the same architect as that of the first one of 1067, the tower has almost 70 different patterns of exquisite decorative brickwork.

1087 Malik Shah arranged the marriage of his daughter and the Abbasid Caliph, al-Moqtadi.

1088 The north domed chamber of the Jame' mosque of Isfahan was constructed under Nezam ol-Molk's archrival at court, the wily Taj ol-Molk.

It shares many of the same formal elements as the southern dome, but is considered more elegant. It is often referred to as the masterpiece of medieval Persian architecture.

1090 Hassan Sabbah was able to seize the great fortress of Alamut in Dailam, a province of the Saljuq empire with the aid of converts.

1090 Hassan Sabbah, founder of Ismaili sect of the Assassins, conquered the stronghold of Alamut fortification, immediately fortifying it further and securing its water supply system.

1092 Malik Shah dispatched troops to besiege Alamut. In a night ambush, the Saljuq troops received heavy casualties and retreated.

1092 Nezam ol-Molk, the celebrated vizier of the Saljuq sultans Alp Arsalan and Malik Shah, was murdered in Sahneh by an Ismaili assassin named Abu Tahir Arrani.

He is best known for his large treatise on kingship, 'Siyasat-nameh' ("the Book of Government"), or Rules for Kings. Nezam ol-Molk was assassinated on the road from Isfahan to Baghdad near Nehavand. The murder was probably committed by an Ismaili from Alamut.

1092 Malik Shah died unexpectedly within weeks of his minister, bringing to an end a glorious epoch.

____ The Saljuq empire began to disintegrate through internal quarrels.

1094 The Fatimid Caliph and Ismaili Imam, al-Mustansir, died.

His death resulted in a division in the Ismaili sect over the question of succession. The heir apparent, Nizar, was stripped of his right to the throne and his younger brother Mosta'la ascended the throne. The consequence was the formation of Nizariyyeh and Mosta'laviyyeh branches of the Ismaili sect.

1095 Pope Urban II advocated a crusade to recover the holy places, at Council of Clermont.

1095 Nizar was killed in prison by his brother, Mosta'la, without leaving a successor.

Hassan Sabbah seized the opportunity and assumed leadership under the title of 'Hojjat–e-Imam', which gave him unquestionable powers in the absence of the Imam.

____ In the Ismaili Doctrine, Ismail, the eldest son of the sixth Imam of the Shias Imam Ja'far Sadiq (A), was appointed as the seventh Imam, but died before his father. Then his son, Mohammad Ibn Ismail, became the ultimate or the "Seventh" Imam; to his followers, the Ismailis, it is he who will return as the absent Imam. Hassan Sabbah's title gave him right of rule on behalf of the Imam.

1096 Sanjar was appointed governor of Khorasan by his half brother Berk-yaruq, who succeeded Malik Shah as sultan. Sanjar in fact acted as an independent prince throughout his reign.

1096 The First Crusade set out.

1097 The crusaders started their military campaigns in Syria.

1097 Sultan Sanjar, the last notable Saljuq monarch, began his rule.

1098 After a long siege crusaders captured the heavily fortified town of Antioch.

1099 Jerusalem fell to the crusaders, and its Muslim and Jewish inhabitants were slaughtered.

1110 The crusaders gained control of a narrow strip of the Palestine coast and established the kingdom of Jerusalem, the county of Tripoli, the principality of Antioch, and the county of Edessa, the so-called crusader states, under various European rulers.

1111 Abu Hamid Mohammad Ghazzali (b.1059), outstanding Muslim theologian, jurist, original thinker, mystic and religious reformer, died.
His great work, 'Revival of the Religious Sciences', made Sufism an acceptable part of orthodox Islam.

____ Sanjar established his suzerainty over the Turkish Qarakhanid princes of Transoxiana and over the Ghaznavids of the Indian borderland.

1117 Sanjar entered Ghazna itself and there installed his own nominee on the throne.

1118 Sultan Sanjar was regarded as the head of the Saljuq house after the death of his full brother Mohammad, the Saljuq king.

1121 Mas'ud Sa'd Salman (b.1046), eminent Persian poet of Lahore, died.

He is famous for the powerful and eloquent laments he wrote from the various places of his eighteen years of imprisonment.

1121 The Jame' mosque of Isfahan was changed to the classical four-ivan type.

1124 Abolfazl Meidani, Arab philologist of Nishapur, died.

He compiled the most comprehensive and most popular collection of classical Arab proverbs, and the only one to be translated into European language (Latin), under the title 'Arabum Proverbia'. He also composed an Arabic-Persian dictionary of common terms and words, and a syntax with Persian notes.

1124 Having appointed Kia Bozorg Ommid as his successor, Hassan Sabbah died.

Hassan Sabbah led a Spartan life, observing the rites of Islam to the full. He is known to have executed his own son, Ostad Hossein, and Zeyd, who had assassinated Da'i Hossein Qa'eni, an Ismaili ruler. The successors followed more pragmatic policies, and managed to establish links with other political powers.

1131 Abolmajd Majdud Ibn Adam Sana'i, one of the most famous poets at the court of the Ghaznavids, died at Ghazna, Afghanistan.

Sana'i's best-known work is the 'Hadiqat al-haqiqah wa shari'at at-tariqah' ("The Garden of Truth and the Law of the Path"), dedicated to Bahram Shah. This great work, expressing the poet's ideas on God, love, philosophy, and reason, is composed of 10,000 couplets in 10 separate sections. Sana'i's work is of major importance in Persian-Islamic literature, for he was the first to use such verse forms as the 'Qasideh' ("ode"), the 'Ghazal' ("lyric"), and the 'masnavi' ("rhymed couplet") to express the philosophical, mystical, and ethical ideas of Sufism. His Divan contains some 30,000 verses.

1132 Omar Khayyam, a brilliant poet and master of philosophy, jurisprudence, history, mathematics, medicine, astronomy, died at 84.

As a scientist, he worked on the reform of the calendar and wrote on algebra and physics. As a poet, he became very popular in the west after Edward Fitzgerald (d.1883) published his free translation of the Robaiyyat. Of the 1,000 quatrains originally attributed to him, 102 are considered authentic, the rest being added in the manuscripts over the course of time.

1134 The Saljuq Empire broke up into two main branches.

The branch of Persian Iraq with its capital at Isfahan and Hamadan that represented the central government of Persia, and the Kerman branch, which was purely local, survived until 1187.

1135 The four-ivan Jame' mosque of Golpayegan was built.

1136 Ismail Ibn Hossein Jorjani, physician who wrote in Arabic and Persian, died.

He composed the first medical encyclopedias in Persian.

1141 Sanjar suffered a terrible defeat near Samarqand at the hands of his new enemy, the recently founded confederacy of Central Asian tribes under the Karakitai.

Transoxiana was lost, and the Karakitai established a distant suzerainty over Khwarezm. Sanjar maintained his hold over Khorasan but he had suffered a great loss of prestige and power.

1141 With the defeat of sultan Sanjar by the Karakitai confederation of northern China, the rulers of Khwarezm were forced to acknowledge the overall sovereignty of the Karakitai.

1144 The Saljuq ruler Zangi, who had established a strong Muslim state at Mosul, captured the city of Edessa from the crusaders.

When news of Edessa's fall reached Europe, Pope Eugenius III called for the Second Crusade.

1147 Gonbad-e Sorkh was built in Maragheh.

This monument with its skillfully designed brick patterns and hefty corner column that recalls the tomb of Ismail Samanid provides a very good example of square based tomb towers. Its secondary ornamentation consists of inset carved terra-cotta panels above the arched panels.

____ There was an uprising of the Oghuz tribes in Sanjar's realm.

1148 Armies from France and Germany joined forces in Jerusalem and with 50,000 crusaders struck north at Damascus.

They began a siege at Damascus but were forced to retreat by an army led by Zangi's successor, Nureddin, and the Second Crusade ended in humiliating failure.

1153 The four-ivan Jame' mosque of Zavareh was built.

1153 Sultan Sanjar was imprisoned by the Oghuz rebels.

They captured the old sultan and kept him prisoner for three years, albeit with respect. He escaped to Merv where he regained the Saljuq throne but died shortly afterwards without having restored order in Khorasan.

Sanjar's three years of imprisonment (1153-1156) was a sad indication of the collapse of the great Saljuq empire.

1155 Nezami Aruzi, one of the most remarkable Persian writers of prose, created his masterwork 'Four Discourses'.

Each of these discourses deals with one of the classes of men whom the author regards as indispensable in the service of kings: secretaries, poets, astrologers and physicians. Nezami also gives the earliest notice of

Ferdowsi, and the only contemporary reference to Omar Khayyam.

1157 Following Sanjar's death, the Khwarezm Shah Ala'eddin Tekish was one of many contenders in a struggle for supremacy in Persia.

On the passing of Saljuq supremacy, southern regions of Persia became independent under the Atabegs, who were originally proxy fathers and tutors accompanying young Saljuq princes who had been sent to govern provinces. At first the atabegs took power in the names of Saljuq puppets. When this fiction lapsed, atabeg dynasties such as the Eldeguzids of Azerbaijan (1137-1225) and Salghurids of Fars (1148-1270) split Persia into independent rival principalities

1166 Abdol Qadir Jilani (b.1077/8) died.

He was a Hanbalite theologian, preacher and Sufi. He gave his name to the mystical order of the Qaderiyyeh. His tomb in Baghdad has remained one of the most frequented sanctuaries of Islam.

1166 Ahmad Yasawi, Muslim saint from Turkestan, died.

He is regarded as having converted the Turks to Islam. Later in the 14th century, Timur (Tamerlane) erected a splendid mausoleum in his honor in the town of Turkestan.

1167 Temujin, who later became known as Genghis Khan, was born.

1167 Oxford University was founded.

1171 Saladin became ruler of Egypt. He superceded the Fatimid dynasty and founded the Ayyubid.

1172 Tekish became the first Khwarezm Shah.

Under Tekish, the Khwarezmians occupied Khorasan, Reyy, and Isfahan.

1177 Toghril III, an energetic and courageous young man, defeated his rival, and sat on the throne as the last Saljuq ruler.

Seventeen years later, in 1194, Toghril III was killed by Tekish.

1180 The four-ivan Jame' mosque of Ardestan was built.

1183 Saladin occupied Aleppo, thus encircling the crusader states.

1184 Sheikh Mosleheddin Sa'di Shirazi, who became one of the greatest figures in classical Persian literature, was born in Shiraz.

1187 Saladin destroyed Jerusalem's army in a battle at Hattin near the Sea of Galilee, and on October 2 captured Jerusalem and most of the other European strongholds.

1191 Sheikh Shahaboddin Sohravardi (b.1155 near Zanjan), also called as-Suhrawardi, mystic theologian and philosopher, died in Aleppo, Syria.

He was a leading figure of the Illuminationist school of Islamic philosophy, attempting to create a synthesis between philosophy and mysticism. He also founded a mystical order known as the Ishraqiyyeh. More than 50 separate works are attributed to Sohravardi. In his best-known work, 'Hikmat ul-ishraq' ("The Wisdom of Illumination"), he said that essences are creations of the intellect, having no objective reality or existence. Concentrating on the concepts of being and non-being, he held that existence is a single continuum that culminates in a pure light that he called God. Other stages of being along this continuum are a mixture of light and dark. While in Syria, his teachings, particularly the pantheistic overtones of his mystical doctrines, aroused the opposition of the established and orthodox Ulama, who persuaded Malik az-Zahir, son of Saladin, to have him put to death.

1192 Richard I, the Lion-Heart, of England negotiated a five-year peace treaty with Saladin that permitted European pilgrims access to holy shrines.

1193 Saladin (b.1137 at Tikrit in Mesopotamia), Muslim Sultan of Egypt, Syria, Yemen, and Palestine, died in Damascus.

He was the founder of the Ayyubid dynasty and the most famous of Muslim heroes. In wars against the Christian crusaders, he achieved final success with the disciplined capture of Jerusalem (Oct. 2, 1187), ending its 88-year occupation by the Franks. The great Christian counterattack of the Third Crusade was then stalemated by his military genius.

1194 Toghril III was killed in the battle of Reyy against Tekish, the first Khwarezm Shah.

1198 Ibn Rushd (b.1126) also called Averroes, Commentator of Aristotle of Cordoba, died in Morocco.

His fields of study were the Qur'anic and natural sciences, including physics, medicine, biology and astronomy, as well as theology and philosophy. Only a small number of his works in Arabic survive, the majority having been preserved in Latin and Hebrew translations.

1199 Afzaloddin Ibrahim Khaqani (b.1126), outstanding Persian poet from Shirvan, died.

He is known for having created a new type of "Qasideh" ("ode") for his panegyrics, but above all for his ascetic Sufi poetry.

1200 Ala'eddin Mohammad Khwarezm Shah ascended the throne and ruled over most of Persia.

Ala'eddin's relations with his neighbors in Central Asia were settled in a more or less satisfactory manner. His neighbors were the Ghurids of Afghanistan; the Qarakhanids of Bukhara; the Karakitai (Qara Khitai) of Yeti-su; the Kuchlug of Naiman tribe; and Genghis Khan, to whom he lost his kingdom piece by piece.

1201 Khajeh Nasireddin Tusi, who became an outstanding scholar and politician, was born in Tus, Khorasan.

1202 Nezami Ganjavi (b.1140), one of the greatest Persian poets and thinkers, died.

Nezami's reputation rests on his great 'Khamseh' ("The Quintuplet"), a pentology of poems written in 'masnavi' verse form ("rhymed couplets") and totaling 30,000 couplets. Drawing inspiration from the Persian epic poets Ferdowsi and Sana'i, he proved himself the first great dramatic poet of Persian literature. The first poem in the pentology is the didactic poem 'Makhzan ol-Asrar' ("The Treasury of Mysteries"), the second the romantic epic 'Khosrow o-Shirin' ("Khosrow and Shirin"). The third is his rendition of a well-known story in Islamic folklore, 'Leili o-Majnun' ("The Story of Leili and Majnun"). The fourth poem, 'Haft Peykar' ("The Seven Beauties"), is considered his masterwork. The final poem in the pentalogy is the 'Eskandarnameh' ("Book of Alexander"), a philosophical portrait of Alexander the Macedonian.

1206 A unified Mongol nation came into existence as the personal creation of Genghis Khan.

Mongol ambitions looked beyond the steppe for the first time. Genghis Khan was ready to start on his great adventure of world conquest. The new nation was organized, above all, for war. Genghis Khan's troops were divided up on the decimal system, were rigidly disciplined, and were well equipped and supplied. The generals were his own sons or picked men, absolutely loyal to him. This was a turning point in the history of the Mongols and in world history.

1207 Mowlana Jalaleddin Rumi, who became the greatest mystic poet in Persian history, was born in Balkh.

1208 Ani, eastern Turkey, was sacked and 12,000 Christians were killed as a result of local campaigns against Georgian princes.

1208 In a violent retribution more than 12,000 citizens of Ardabil were slain.

1209 Fakhreddin Razi (b.1149 in Reyy), Muslim theologian and scholar, died near Herat.

He was the author of one of the most authoritative commentaries on the Qur'an in the history of Islam. His intellectual brilliance was universally acclaimed and attested by such works as 'Mafatih ol-ghayb' ("The Keys to the Unknown") or 'Kitab at-tafsir al-kabir' ("The Great Commentary") and 'Muhassal afkar ol-mutaqaddimin wa-al-muta`akhkhirin' ("Collection of the Opinions of Ancients and Moderns").

1209 Cambridge University was founded.

1210 University of Paris was founded.

1211 Genghis Khan fell upon the Chin empire of north China.

1215 Genghis Khan sacked Peking, the capital of China.

1215 King John of England was forced by the English barons to accept a political charter known as the Magna Carta, which granted certain political and civil liberties as the fundamental principles of the British Constitution.

1217 The robbery and murder of a caravan of merchants from Mongolia by customs officials of sultan Mohammad Khwarezm Shah at Otrar, now Shymkent in Kazakhstan, triggered Genghis Khan to attack Persia.

1219 Genghis Khan conquered Bukhara.
This is known as the first Mongol invasion.

1220 Genghis Khan conquered Samarqand.
Soon after the fall of Samarqand he dispatched his elder sons north into Khwarezm to lay siege to Mohammad's capital. He now sent his youngest son into eastern Persia to sack and destroy the great and populous cities of Merv and Neishabur.

1220 Genghis Khan's son, Tolui, invaded Khorasan.

____ Sultan Jalaleddin, the son of Sultan Mohammad, made his way into central Afghanistan and inflicted a defeat on a Mongol force at Parvan, north of Kabul.

1221 Genghis Khan, rejoined by his sons, defeated this new adversary on the banks of the Indus River.
With Jalaleddin's defeat the campaign in the west was virtually brought to its conclusion, and Genghis Khan

proceeded by easy stages on the long journey back to Mongolia.

1221 **Genghis Khan generals, Jebe and Subetei, explored the area round the Caspian Sea.**

The famous Arab historian Ibn al-Athir (d.1234) remarks that for some years he refrained from mentioning this event, which he later described as 'the greatest catastrophe and the most dire calamity' that had ever overtaken mankind.

The Persian historian Joveini (1226-1283) relates that after the capture of a city the population was slaughtered, each Mongol soldier being made responsible for the execution of several hundred persons.

1227 **Genghis Khan died.**

He died in August in his summer quarters in the district of Qingshui, south of the Liupan Shan (Liupan Mountains) in Gansu, China.

1230 **The Mongol Chormaghan managed to put an end to the adventures of Jalaleddin Khwarezm Shah.**

1231 **Jalaleddin Khwarezm Shah, who had fled before the Mongols to the Caspian area, died.**

1236 Cordoba was conquered by Christians.

1240 Mongols occupied Kiev and all of Russia.

1242 **The Mongol Baiju completed the Mongol conquests, pushing on deep into Asia Minor.**

Immediately after the conquest, the Mongol administrators arrived to rebuild the conquered cities and establish some kind of order. As in the times of the Seleucids, the Arabs and the Saljuqs, Persian functionaries again collaborated with the invaders and helped them to restore order in the country.

1247 **Shams Tabrizi, Sufi from Tabriz, disappeared forever.**

He was the spiritual guide of Mowlana Rumi.

1248 Christians conquered Seville.

1250 Mamluk dynasty was founded in Egypt.

Mamluks were originally a group of slave soldiers under the Ayyubid dynasty. Mamluk generals used their power to establish a dynasty that ruled Egypt and Syria.

1251 **At a grand council held in Mongolia, it was decided that a brother of the Great Khan, Qubilai, should go to China and another brother, Hulagu, to Persia as imperial lieutenants.** Hulagu, a grandson of Genghis Khan, was given the task of capturing Persia by the paramount Mongol chieftain Mongke.

1253 Hulagu set out with a Mongol army of about 130,000.

1253 Safieddin Ardabili, who became a great Sufi Sheikh, was born in Ardabil.

1254 Probable birth date of Marco Polo, who became an adventurer-merchant and outstanding traveler.

Mongol Period

1256 – 1383

In the early 13th century, the Mongol empire, under the leadership of Genghis Khan, grew out of their origional homeland in the eastern zone of the Asian steppe, savagely wiped out towns and villages, left endless trails of devestation, and created the greatest catastrophy that had ever overtaken mankind, and dominated most of Asia. After the death of Genghis khan, the empire was divided among his heirs. Having captured Baghdad and all Iran, Hulagu khan, son of Genghis khan, founded the Il-Khanid dynasty. The Il-Khans consolidated their position in Iran and reunited the region as a political and territorial entity after centuries of fragmented rule by local dynasties. Under Persian influence, the Mongols eventually converted to Islam, and encouraged development of the arts and sciences. New systems of taxation were introduced, armed forces were reformed and communications reorganized. When the last khan died without a male heir in 1335, the territory broke up into small states ruled mainly by Iranians.

1256 Mongol Commander Hulagu crossed Oxus, took possession of his domains, and assumed ruling the western part of the Mongol Empire, known as the
Il-Khanid Empire.

1256 Hulagu Khan seized the Castle of Alamut, Ismaili stronghold, and put an end to the assassins.
He seized and imprisoned the leader of the Ismailis in Qazvin, invaded the fortress, and massacred its inhabitants. The community did not die out completely, but scattered throughout the country. We will hear of the Ismailis again in 1770, when, with the blessing of the Zand family, they were in control of the cities of Kerman and Bam.

1257 Hulagu Khan chose Maragheh as his capital.
Maragheh was rich in rivers and pastures, and bore some resemblance to Mongolia.

1257 Sheikh Ajal Sa'di Shirazi completed his great literary work, Bustan ("The Orchard").

____ Hulagu defeated the Caliph's army and captured and executed al-Musta'sim, the last of the Abbasid Caliphs

1258 Hulagu Khan began his devastating assault on Baghdad, and ended 525 years of the Abbasid Caliphate.
He took Khajeh Nasireddin Tusi, the renowned astronomer and politician of his time, as a confidant.
The mainstay of Muslim orthodoxy, the Abbasid Caliph was captured and disgracefully put to death.

1258 Sa'di Shirazi completed his masterpiece, Golestan ("The Rose Garden").

____ Sa'di dedicated his celebrated works, Bustan and Golestan, to the Atabeg Abu Bakr of Fars.

1260 Hulagu captured Syria but was decisively defeated by the Egyptian army.

1265 Abagha ascended the Il-Khanid throne in Persia after the death of Hulagu.

1268 The Christians lost Antioch.

1273 **Mowlana Jalaleddin Rumi, the founder of the Mowlaviyyeh order of Sufism (The Whirling Dervishes), died at 66.**

He is most famous for his lyrics and for his didactic epic 'Masnavi-ye Ma'navi' (Spiritual Couplets), which widely influenced Muslim mystical thought and literature.

1274 **Khajeh Nasireddin Tusi, a Persian astronomer of exceptionally wide scholarship, died in Baghdad.**

Tusi, taking advantage of his position as head of the ministry of religious bequests, had a fine observatory built in Maragheh. He wrote many books in Arabic and Persian, and improved upon earlier Arabic translations of Euclid, Ptolemy, Autolycus, Theodosius, Apollonius, and others. He also made original contributions to mathematics and astronomy: his 'Zij Ilkhani' is a splendidly accurate table of planetary movements. His 'Tajrid al-aqa'id' is a highly esteemed treatise on Shi'i dogmatics. His most famous and popular work is the 'Akhlaq Naseri', a treatise on ethics in the Greek tradition drawing upon the 11th-century 'Tahzib al-khlaq' of Ibn Meskavayh, which he drafted while a prisoner of the Assassins and later revised for his Mongol master. This work has been translated into English.

1275 **Abaqa Khan built a palace on the ruins of a site already sacred to the Sassanians, Takht-e Soleiman, or The Throne of Solomon, centred on a perpetual lake in the crater of an extinct volcano.**

1282 **Upon the death of Il-Khan Abagha, his son Prince Arghun was a candidate for the throne but was forced to yield to a stronger rival, his uncle Teguder.**

____ **Arghun accused Teguder's followers of having poisoned his father and protested Teguder's conversion to Islam.**

1283 **Alaeddin Joveini (b.1226), Persian governor and historian from Jovein in Neishabur, died.**

He visited Mongolia, accompanied the Mongol Il-Khan Hulegu on his campaigns against the Ismailis of Alamut and the Baghdad Caliphate, and saved the famous library of

Alamut from destruction. He wrote a history of the Mongols and of the dynasty of the Kharazm Shahs, which has considerably influenced historical tradition in the East and is a historical authority of first rank.

1284 **Arghun was enthroned, and as an ardent Buddhist countermanded the Islamic policies of his predecessor.**
Arghun, as the head of rebellion against Teguder, succeeded in overthrowing him and having him executed.

1284 **Arghun appointed his 13-year-old son Ghazan viceroy of the provinces of northeastern Persia.**
Ghazan resided in that area for the next 10 years and defended the frontier against the Chagatai Mongols of Central Asia and then against his own lieutenant Nowruz, who had risen in revolt with the Chagatai.

1285 **Arghun sought alliances with the Christian West, writing to Pope Honorius IV in hopes of renewing the war against the Egyptian Mamluks.**

1287 **Arghun sent emissaries to such leaders as Pope Nicholas IV, Edward I of England, and Philip IV of France.**
Except for an exchange of letters, nothing came of this diplomacy, and the war against Egypt was not resumed.

1289 **Arghun appointed an anti-Islamic Jew, Sa'd od-Dowleh, first as his minister of finance and then as vizier of his entire empire.**
The predominantly Muslim population may have resented the rule of a Buddhist and a Jew, but their administration proved lawful and just and restored order and prosperity.

1289 The Christians lost Tripoli.

1290 **The Radekan tomb tower was constructed.**
This provides a very good example of an important group of tomb towers in which the body of the tower is composed of an engaged cluster of almost round shafts, where the circular shafts alternate with prismatic flanges and both are elaborately ornamented.

1291 While Arghun was dying, fevered and bedridden, the factions opposed to Sa'd od-Dowleh rose up and put Arghun and his minister to death.

1291 Gaykhatu, Arghun's brother, came to the Il-Khanid throne.

1291 Sheikh Mosleheddin Sa'di Shirazi, the outstanding Persian poet, died at 107 in Shiraz.

He acquired the traditional learning of Islam at the Nezamiyeh madrassa in Baghadad. The unsettled conditions following the Mongol invasion of Persia led him to wander abroad through Anatolia, Syria, Egypt, and Iraq. He refers in his work to travels in India and Central Asia, but these cannot be confirmed. In North Africa, he was held captive by the Franks and put to work in the trenches of the fortress of Tripoli. He was an elderly man when he reappeared in his native Shiraz, where he is said to have spent the rest of his life.

1291 The fall of Acre marked the end of Christian power in Syria and Palestine.

1295 Baydu, Gaykhatu's cousin, dethroned him and usurped the Il-Khanid throne.

1295 Ghazan defeated and deposed Baydu.

After a first encounter, followed by a truce, Ghazan spent the summer in the mountains north of present-day Tehran, where he adopted 'Mahmud' as his name and declared himself a convert to Islam on the advice of Nowruz, with whom he was now reconciled. His example was followed by the troops under his command. It was thus as the head of a Muslim force that he resumed the attack against Baydu, who, deserted by his supporters, was captured and executed on the very day of Ghazan's entry into the new Il-Khanid capital of Tabriz.

Ghazan Khan introduced profound social and administrative changes that were to have a lasting impact on the future systems of government.

____ **Ghazan Khan suppressed a number of revolts against his authority.**

No fewer than five princes of the blood were executed for their complicity. Nowruz himself, who had helped raise Ghazan to the throne, was soon to pay with his life for suspected collusion with the Mamluks.

1298 **Yaqut al-Musta'simi, famous calligrapher, died.**

He composed an anthology and a collection of aphorisms.

1298 **Rashideddin (b.ca.1247), the greatest statesman of his time, became vizier to Ghazan Khan.**

He was perhaps the real author of the fiscal reforms that went under his master's name

1300 **Ghazan Khan invaded Syria, defeated the Egyptian army at Homs, and made a triumphal entry into Damascus.**

Upon his return to Persia, however, Syria was re-occupied by the Mamluks.

1301 **Sheikh Zahid Gilani, for 25 years the master of Sheikh Safieddin Ardabili, died at 85.**

With his death Sheikh Safieddin took over the Zahidiyyeh order and transformed it into his own Safavid Sufi order.

1304 **Ghazan Khan died due to illness and his brother, Oljeitu, began to rule.**

During Ghazan Khan's reign, the Il-Khans lost all contact with the remaining Mongol chieftains of China. His reign also saw a Persian cultural renaissance in which scholars like Rashideddin flourished under his patronage.

Oljeitu was baptized a Christian and given the name Nicholas by his mother. As a youth, he converted to Buddhism and later to the Sunni branch of Islam, taking the name Mohammad Khodabandeh.

____ **Oljeitu moved the Il-Khanid capital from Tabriz to Soltaniyyeh.**

1309 **Oljeitu converted to Shi'ism.**

1310 **Greatly influenced by the Iraqi Shia theologian Ibn al-Mutahhar al-Hilli, a pupil of Khajeh Nasireddin Tusi, Oljeitu**

embraced Shi'ism and on his return from a visit to the tomb of Imam Ali (A) in Iraq (1309-10), he proclaimed Shia Islam to be the state religion of Persia.

1310 The magnificent stucco mihrab in the Jame mosque of Isfahan was made.

The inscriptions, made and signed by Haidar, a pupil of the distinguished calligrapher Yaqut al-Musta'simi, mention the names of the twelve Shia imams, artistically decorated with floral motifs, and that might be a n indication of Oljeitu's conversion to Shi'ism.

1311 Qotboddin Shirazi (b.1236), Persian astronomer and physician, died.

In his two comprehensive astronomical works he has given what is conceivably the best Arabic account of astronomy (cosmography) with the help of mathematics.

1312 Oljeitu pursued the traditional hostility between the Il-Khans and the Mamluks with a badly organized invasion of Mamluk territory. The expedition had to be abandoned after the expected help from European princes failed to materialize.

1313 Tomb tower at Bastam was built.

The facade of this monument, like that of Gonbad-e Qabus, comprises prismatic flanges.

1313 The mausoleum of Oljeitu, Iran's Taj Mahal, was completed at Sultaniyeh.

This typically Mongol style octagonal mausoleum is one of Iran's supreme architectural achievements. The 53 m (177 ft) high and 24 m (80 ft) in diameter dome, solidly covered with light blue faience tile, rests on a wide and rich stalactite cornice. Eight embellished minarets with blue patterns rise from the corners of the building and surround the dome. The monument reflects both the Dome of the Rock, and in its location in the open countryside, the nomadic tents of Turko-Mongol tribes.

1316 Il-Khan Oljeitu died, and his son Il-Khan Abu Sa'id ascended the throne.

____ Abu Sa'id reconverted to Sunni Islam and thus averted the unrest among Sunnis caused by Oljeitu's conversion to Shi'ism.
During his reign, factional disputes and internal disturbances became rampant.

1318 Rashideddin, Persian statesman and historian, and the author of a universal history, died.
He became vizier to Ghazan in 1298 and served under his successor Oljeitu.
Accused by his rivals of having poisoned his sovereign, he was put to death by Oljeitu's son Abu Sa'id.
Rashideddin's history, 'Jame at-tawarikh', covers realms even beyond the Muslim world.

1320 Mahmud Shabestari (b.ca.1250 in Shabestar near Tabriz), Persian mystic and writer, died.
His fame rests entirely on his poem in rhyming couplets, called 'Golshan Raaz' ("The Rose Garden of the Secret").
Golshan Raaz, written in 1311 or possibly 1317, is a poetical expression of Shabestari's retreat from the temporal world.
It consists of questions and answers about mystical doctrines.

1324 Khajeh Mohammad Shirazi, who was to acquire the title 'Hafez' and become a great Persian lyric poet and panegyrist, was born in Shiraz.
The title of 'Hafez' is given to anyone who can recite the whole Qur'an by heart.

1324 Marco Polo died in Venice.
From 1271 to 1295 he journeyed from Europe to China through Persia. He remained in China for 17 of those years.
His 'Il milione' ("The Million"), known in English as the 'Travels of Marco Polo', became a geographical classic.

1330 Shah Nematollah Vali was born in Syria.

1334 Sheikh Safieddin Ardabili, the renowned mystic and founder of the Safavid Sufi order, died at 81 in Ardabil.

Popularity of the Safavid order was attributed in part to Safieddin's policy of hospitality, especially to all who sought refuge. One of the sheikh's appellations was Khalil-e Ajam (the Persian Abraham, who is noted for hospitality in Persian folklore).

1335 Il-Khan Abu Sa'id, the last notable Mongol ruler, died without leaving an heir.

With his death, the unity of the dynasty was fractured. Thereafter, various Il-Khanid princes ruled as regional authorities until 1353.

1336 Timur (Tamerlane), who later became a celebrated Turkic conqueror of Islamic faith, was born at Kish, near Samarqand.

Timur was a member of a Mongol subgroup that had settled in Transoxiana (now roughly corresponding to Uzbekistan) after taking part in Genghis Khan's son Chagatai's campaigns in that region. Timur thus grew up in what was known as the Chagatai khanate.

1337 Abd ur-Razzaq led the democratic movement of Sarbedaran against the oppression of Mongol tax collectors.

A former functionary of Persian origin, Abd ur-Razzaq founded a popular republic led by cable men who had risen against Mongol rule from their center at Sabzevar in Khorasan, and spread out to Neishabur and Mazandaran.

1339 Hamd Allah Mostowfi Qazvini, Persian historian and geographer from Qazvin, died.

His work is important for the period of the Il-Khans.

1339 New centers of power were asserting their independence after the decline of the Il-Khans.

____ Two of the notable dynasties that emerged were All-e-Jalayer , or the Jalalyrids, in Baghdad and Syria, and All-e-Mozaffar, or the Mozaffarids, in Shiraz, Isfahan, Kerman and Yazd.

1347 The first onset of the Black Death, pandemic of plague, ravaged Europe for five years.

It took a proportionately greater toll of life than any other known epidemic or war up to that time.

1352 Kamaleddin Khaju Kermani (b.1290), Persian poet, died in Shiraz.

1366 Having defeated the governor of Transoxiana, Timur achieved firm possession of that region.

1368 Ibn Battuta (b.1304 in Tanjiers, Morocco), one of the world's most renowned travelers and authors of travel books, died.

His 'Travel-book' is in fact a description of the then known world, and has been translated into many languages.

1368 Ibn Yamin (b.1287), the most important Persian poet of epigrams, died.

He was one of the earliest poets to write on the Shia Imams and the tragedy of Karbala.

1370 Timur proclaimed himself sovereign of the Chagatai line of khans and restorer of the Mongol Empire in Samarqand.

1371 Obeyd Zakani (b.1300), Persian poet from Qazvin, died.

He was a satirical and erotic poet, who wrote such works as 'The Morals of Aristocracy' and 'The Book of the Beard', a dialogue between the poet and the beard, regarded as a destroyer of youthful beauty.

Timurid Period

1383 – 1501

Timurid dynasty was founded by Tamerlane, a Turkic ruler and conqueror, whose far-flung expeditions carried him from southern Russia to India and from Central Asia to Turkey. Tamerlane ruled Samarqand as his capital, enriching the city and surrounding region with the loot of his campaigns. From the region's mixed population, Tamerlane organized an efficient army of infantry, engineers, and cavalry, and over the next ten years began to expand his control over surrounding territory. Tamerlane and his successors built many spectacular palaces and mosques, and are noted for their patronage of scholarship, arts, Turkish and Persian literature, and revival of artistic and intellectual life in Iran and Central Asia.

1383 Timur began his conquests in Persia with the capture of Herat.
The Persian political and economic situation was extremely precarious. The signs of recovery visible under the later Mongol rulers suffered a setback after the death of Abu Sa'id in 1335. The vacuum of power was filled by rival dynasties, torn by internal dissensions and unable to put up resistance.

1385 Khorasan and all eastern Persia fell to Timur.

1385 Timur's palace was founded at Kish, his birthplace in Central Asia.
It was not quite finished 20 years later, when Clavijo, the ambassador of Henry III, king of Castile, saw it in 1405. No monarch in Asia could boast of anything comparable.

1389 Khajeh Bahaeddin Naqshband (b.1318), a renowned Sufi leader, died.
He founded the important and still active Naqshbandiyyeh Sufi order. In the extent of its diffusion, this order has been second only to the Qaderiyyeh.

1390 Hafez, commonly considered the pre-eminent master of the Ghazal form, died in Shiraz.

1390 The Qara Quyunlu ("Black Sheep") Turkmens, who already had under their control an area close to Lake Van and mountainous regions in Armenia, annexed Azerbaijan.

1391 Sheikh Sadreddin (b.1305), son of Sheikh Safieddin, died.
He constructed the Safavid family mausoleum from 1324 to 1334. During his 57 years as head of the order, he witnessed the collapse of the Mongols.

1393 Timur conquered Baghdad.

1394 Timur became master of Fars, Iraq, Azerbaijan, Armenia, Mesopotamia, and Georgia, the regions he had conquered between 1386 and 1394.

1396 Timur appointed his son, Shahrokh, as ruler of Eastern Persia.
Shahrokh had two wives, Gowharshad and Malikat.

1397 Umar al-Khalwati, founder of the highly diversified and widespread mystical order of Khalwatiyyeh, died.

1398 Timur invaded India on the pretext that the Muslim sultans of Delhi were showing excessive tolerance to their Hindu subjects.

He crossed the Indus River and, leaving a trail of carnage, marched on Delhi. The army of the Delhi sultan was destroyed, and Delhi was reduced to ruins, from which it took more than a century to emerge.

1399 Timur set out on his last great expedition, to punish the Mamluk sultan of Egypt and the Ottoman sultan Bayazid I for their seizures of certain of his territories.

1400 Geoffrey Chaucer (b.ca.1343), the father of English poetry, died. His best-known work is The Canterbury Tales.

1401 Having restored his control over Azerbaijan, Timur marched on Syria; Aleppo was stormed and sacked, the Mamluk army defeated, and Damascus occupied.

1401 Timur conquered Baghdad.

20,000 of its citizens were massacred, and all its monuments were destroyed.

1402 Having wintered in Georgia, Timur invaded Anatolia and destroyed Bayazid's army near Ankara.

____ Timur received offers of submission from the sultan of Egypt and from John VII (then co-emperor of the Byzantine Empire with Manuel II Palaeologus).

1402 Timur met the Sufi Khajeh Ali in Ardabil on the way back to Central Asia.

Khajeh Ali left so great an impression on him that he is said to have donated land to the shrine. Timur also issued decrees to exempt Sufi orders from tax, and to guarantee their safety.

1404 Timur returned to Samarqand and prepared for an expedition to China.

1404 The mosque of Bibi Khanum in Samarqand was completed after 6 years of construction.

The whole building, including its eight minarets and three domes, was covered with enameled tiles.

1405 Timur fell ill on his expedition to China and died at Otrar in February.

His body was embalmed, laid in an ebony coffin, and sent to Samarqand, where it was buried in the sumptuous tomb called Gur-e Amir ("Tomb of the Commander").

____ Timur's conquests were divided between two of his sons: Miranshah received Iraq, Azerbaijan, Moghan, Shirvan, and Georgia, while Shahrokh was left with Khorasan.

1406 Abd ur-Rahman Ibn Khaldun (b.1332), historian, sociologist and philosopher of Tunis, died.

He is one of the strongest personalities of Arabo-Muslim culture in the period of its decline.

1407 Miranshah died and Shahrokh became the undisputed king of Persia, Armenia, Georgia and Baghdad, and installed his son, Ulugh Beg, as governor of Samarqand while he remained in Herat.

1416 Gowharshad ordered extensive renovations to the shrine of Imam Reza (A), the eighth Shia Imam, in Mashad.

The purpose behind this project was primarily to satisfy the increasingly influential Shia community in Persia. She added a large Jame' mosque and two assembly halls, Dar al-Siyada ("House for Sayyids") and Dar al-Huffaz ("House for Reciters"), to the pre-existing complex to accommodate the growing number of pilgrims.

____ The architect Qavamoddin Shirazi used the traditional four-ivan plan for the mosque, but ingeniously placed a dome over, not beyond, the Qibla ivan.

The mosque's Qibla ivan was distinguished by flanking minarets with lozenge decoration and a broad inscription band in tile mosaic, personally designed by Gowharshad's son Baysonghor, a renowned calligrapher and the leading bibliophile of the day.

1417 Shahrokh's son, Ulugh Beg, built a royal madrasa and Khaneqah facing the Ragistan, the town square of Samarqand.

1417 Gowharshad began a large complex in Herat.
It took two decades (1417-1438) for Qavamoddin Shirazi, the same architect Gowharshad had hired to work in Mashad, to complete the work which included a large rectangular Jame' mosque and a madrasa with a dynastic mausoleum. He ingeniously used an elaborate system of squinch-net vaulting in the Mausoleum that proves to be the most important innovation in Timurid architecture. Today only two minarets and the tomb, covered with the typical Timurid high double dome, remain.

1417 Shahrokh crushed local warlords and rebellious nephews attempting to seize control of Isfahan region.

1427 Khajeh Ali, who for the first time used Shia doctrine in the teachings of Safavid mystic order, died.

1427 Shahrokh was the target of an assassination attempt. Stabbed in the stomach when leaving the Friday prayer, he made a full recovery.

1429 Ghiyasoddin Kashani, mathematician and astronomer, died.
He wrote in Persian and Arabic. He assisted in establishing Ulugh Beg's astronomical tables, and worked out the value of Đ (pi=3.14) with extraordinary precision.

1430 Hafez Abru, Persian historian of the Timurid period and documenter of the reign of Shahrokh, died.

1431 Shah Nematollah Vali, Persian mystic and eponym of the Nematollahiyyeh order of Sufism, died.
He was a descendent of the fifth Imam of Shia. He is highly esteemed in Persia as a great saint and miracle-worker, and his tomb at Mahan is a popular place of pilgrimage. The order was reintroduced into Persia in the late 18th century and became the most widely spread Sufi order in the country.

1435 Abdul Qadir Gheibi died.

He was the greatest of the Persian writers on music; his works are of great importance in the history of Persian, Arabian and Turkish music.

1436 The Shrine of Shah Nematollah Vali was built in Mahan under the patronage of his Indian disciple, Ahmad Shah Dakani.

1437 Mir Chakhmaq complex was founded in Yazd.
This complex was built under the patronage of Shahrokh's governor, Mir Chakhmaq, and his wife. It included a four-ivan mosque, Khaneqah, qanat, cistern, and well, supported by a nearby bath house and caravanserai.

1440 German craftsman Johan Gutenberg invented a method of printing from movable type, used almost unchanged until the 20th century.

1444 The Ghiasiyyeh madrasa was built at Khargird in Khorasan province.
The architecture of this building reflects the height of the new types of vaults in early Timurid architecture. This is Qavamoddin's last work which was finished by his pupil, Ghiyasoddin Shirazi. Here one can find the elaboration of entrance complex as an architectural unit, which is a main characteristic of Timurid architecture.

1444 Shahrokh fell seriously ill, and Gowharshad, his wife, was promoted as the rightful heir apparent. His health improved.

1447 Sheikh Ebrahim, under whose leadership the Safavid Sufi order acquired exceptional wealth and influence, died.

1447 Shahrokh died.
During Shahrokh's reign, economic prosperity was restored and much of the damage wrought by Timur's campaigns was repaired. Trading and artistic communities were brought into the capital city of Herat, where a library was founded, and the capital became the center of a renewed and artistically brilliant Persian culture.

1453 Ottomans conquered the Byzantine capital of Constantinople. Mehmed the conqueror ordered the great Byzantine imperial church of Haghia Sophia ("Holy Wisdom") to be transformed into the city's congregational mosque.

1454 Sharafeddin Yazdi, Persian poet and historian, died. He wrote the history of Timur.

1454 The Darb-e Imam mausoleum was built in Isfahan. This shrine has an exquisite tile mosaic portal which is one of the finest examples of decorated architecture in Persia, with symmetrically displayed panels containing arabesques, vases, and inscriptions that describe the building.

1457 Gowharshad, the formidable wife of king Shahrokh, died. After her death the house of Timur fell and the empire was fragmented.

1460 Sultan Jonaid, also known as Sheikh Joneid, was killed in battle.
He was the Sheikh of the Safavid Sufi order who for the first time used the title of Sultan instead of Sheikh. The title of Sultan denoted his leadership's military might and political ambition.

1465 The 'Kabud' ("Blue") mosque was built in Tabriz. The mosque, which takes its name from the superb tile revetment, was originally part of a multi functional complex, known as the Muzaffariyyeh after its patron Abol Muzaffar Jahanshah. The complex included a cistern, library, tomb, and Khaneqah for Sufis, but the identification of the surviving part is unclear.

1467 Aq Quyunlu ("White Sheep") Turkmens formed a dynasty under Ozun Hassan.

1481 The Spanish Inquisition was established.

1482 Abd ur-Razzaq Samarqandi (b.1413), a Persian historian, died.
He served several Timurid rulers in Samrakand and left an important source of historical information.

1487 Ismail, who became the founder of the Safavid dynasty and Shah of Persia, was born.
Ismail was the son of Sultan Heidar and Martha.
Sultan Heidar (d.1488) was the son of Sultan Jonaid and Khajeh Beigom, Ozun Hassan's sister.
Martha (Almashah Beigom) was the daughter of Ozun Hassan and Dezpina, daughter of Kalo Yohans, ruler of Trabozan.

1488 Sultan Heidar, Ismail's father and head of a Shia group known as the Qizilbash ("Red Heads"), was killed in battle against the Sunni king of Shirvan.
Fearful that the Sunnis, the majority sect, would wipe out the entire family, Shia supporters kept Ismail's family members hidden for a number of years.

1490 Khajeh Obeidollah Ahrar (b.1404), sheikh of Naqshbandiyyeh order of Sufism, died.
Under his guidance, the order became firmly rooted in Central Asia.

1490 Galatasaray, palace school in Galata, Turkey, was founded.

1492 Italian explorer Christopher Columbus (1451-1506) discovered the West Indies.

1492 Mowlana Nureddin Jami (b.1414), great Persian poet and mystic, died in Herat, Afghanistan.
He is often regarded as the last mystical poet of Persia. His most famous collection of poetry is a seven-part compendium entitled 'Haft Owrang' ("The Seven Thrones").

1497 Vasco da Gama, Portuguese navigator, made his first voyage to India. In this way he opened up the sea route from western Europe to the East by way of the Cape of Good Hope and thus ushered in a new era in world history.

1501 Ismail emerged at the age of 14 to take his father's position as head of the Qizilbash. He quickly established a base of power in northwestern Persia.

1501 Ismail defeated and killed Farrokh Yasar, king of Shirvan.

1501 Leading an army of 7,000, Ismail confronted an army of 30,000 Aq Quyunlu men whom he managed to crush.

Safavid Period

1501 – 1736

During the 15th century, several competing families and tribes, mostly of Turkic origins, ruled over various parts of Iran. Notable among them were the Safavids, who headed a militant Sufi order founded in the northwest by Shaikh Safi of Ardabil. His descendant, Ismail I, conquered first Tabriz and then the rest of Iran, and in 1501 proclaimed himself shah, a title commonly used by Iranian rulers in pre-Islamic times. This marked the beginning of the Safavid dynasty and was the first time since the 7th century that all of Iran was unified as an independent state. Ismail embraced Jafari Shia Islam, established it as the state religion, and began to convert the largely Sunni population to this Shia sect. The Safavids, namely Shah Abbas, made great contribution to education, commerce, urban development and architectural beauty of Persia.

1501 Having defeated his main enemies, Ismail entered the Aq Quyunlu capital city of Tabriz and crowned himself king of Persia.

At this time, Persia was divided into several local governments and principalities of predominantly Sunni faith which inevitably would have fallen to the Sunni-dominated Ottoman Empire had it not been for Ismail. To reshape and unite the nation, and to create a religious rift between Persians and non-Persians (especially the Ottomans), Shah Ismail proclaimed Shi'ism as the state religion. He enforced this new policy with intense religious intolerance, putting to the sword all those resisting conversion to Shi'ism.

1504 Kamaleddin Hossein Kashefi, Persian writer and preacher, died.

Among other works, he wrote a new Persian version of 'Kalila va Dimna'. The Ottoman Turkish translation of this work became widely known in Europe; its translation into French is one of the sources of La Fontaine's 'Fables'.

1514 Crown Prince Tahmasb was born.

1514 Shah Ismail was defeated at the battle of Chalderan by the Ottoman Sultan Salim.

The two sides were unequal in terms of military strength. The Ottoman army, three times the size of the Persian army, was supported by artillery. Tabriz fell to the Ottomans, but due to the extreme cold, they were logistically unable to hold it for more than eight days.

____ The Portuguese fleet under Tristan da Cunha attacked and occupied the Island of Hormuz in the Persian Gulf.

This marked the beginning of almost a century of Portuguese domination over that area.

1515 The Portuguese General, Alberquerque, built a castle on the Island of Hormuz.

1519 Leonardo da Vinci (b.1452), Italian artist, scientist and writer, died. He was a great painter, engineer, mathematician, musician, naturalist, philosopher, architect and sculptor of the Renaissance.

1521 The Portuguese seized Bahrain.

1521 Ferdinand Magellan (b.ca.1480), Portuguese sailor, died.

1524 Vasco da Gama (b.1460), Portuguese navigator, died in his last voyage to India. He helped make Portugal a world power.

1524 Shah Ismail died, and the 10-year-old Crown Prince Tahmasb was placed on the Safavid throne.

1527 Nicolo Machiavelli (b.1469), Italian politician and author, died.

1530 Shah Tahmasb had his world famous Shahnameh created. This monumental two-volume copy of Shahnameh, the Persian national epic, had 742 pages of poetry and 258 exquisite illustrations painted over a decade by many of the finest artists.

1536 Kamaleddin Behzad (b.ca.1450), the most famous Persian miniature-painter, died.
His patrons were the poet Mir Ali Shir Nava'I; the Timurid ruler in Khorasan, Hossein Bayqara; and the Safavid shahs Ismail and Tahmasb. His students included the painters Qasim Ali, Mir Seyyed Ali, Aqa Mirak and Mozaffar Ali.

1539 The famous silken Ardabil Carpet, world renowned for its design and workmanship, was made for the Ardabil mosque by order of Shah Tahmasb.
The Ardabil Carpet is now kept in the Victoria and Albert Museum in London, and its twin is in the Los Angeles County Museum of Art.

1543 Nicolas Copernicus (b.1473), Polish astronomer, died. He was the first European to suggest that the earth and other planets moved around the sun and that the earth was not the center of the universe.

1546 Bahaeddin Mohammad Hossein Ameli (Sheikh Baha'i) was born in Baalbak, Syria.

He became a great theologian, mathematician, jurist and astronomer of the Safavid court.

1555 Shah Tahmasb signed the peace treaty of Amasiyyeh with the Ottomans.

The treaty followed four attempts by the Ottoman Suleyman the Great (r.1520-1566) to conquer Persian territory. As a result of this treaty, little land exchanged hands except for Georgia, which was divided between the two countries.

1555 Shah Tahmasb moved the capital from Tabriz to Qazvin, away from Ottoman reach.

Only a portal and a restored pavilion from his palace have survived the numerous earthquakes.

1564 Michelangelo (b.1475), Italian sculptor, painter, architect and poet, died.

1570 Reza Abbasi, who became a great Persian painter, was born in Mashad.

1571 Molla Sadra, who was to lead the Persian cultural renaissance as a great philosopher, was born in Shiraz.

1571 Abbas, the third son of Mohammad Khodabandeh, was born.

1576 Shah Tahmasb died.

During his 52 years of powerful reign, he managed to restore order in the country. His greatest achievement was in keeping the Ottomans back in the Caucasus. His conquests provided him with considerable wealth and numerous slaves and man-power needed for the special regiments of the Persian army.

1576 Ismail II (b.1536), having been released from his father's prison after twenty years, placed himself on the Safavid throne.

____ Ismail II mercilessly put most of the princes and his father's officials to death.

1578 Ismail II was murdered by those fearing their execution.

1578 Ismail II's brother, Mohammad Khodabandeh, was declared the Safavid king.

He had escaped execution together with his three sons, Hamzeh, Abutalib and Abbas. During Sultan Mohammad Shah's reign, power was mostly in the hands of his elder sons, Hamzeh and Abutalib, as well as the powerful Qizilbash Chieftains, who were constantly trying to undermine the power of the king.

1587 Sultan Mohammad Shah was forced to abdicate in favor of his 17-year-old son, Abbas, who had successfully led a coup against him.

Sultan Mohammad Shah, an almost totally blind Sultan of little authority, was incompetent in running the country. His legacy was an amalgamation of internal crisis and foreign invasions. The Uzbeks were attacking the northeast while the Ottomans were invading the west and northwest.

1587 Abbas came to the throne.

This was a critical moment in the fortunes of the Safavid dynasty.

To deal with the Qizilbash Chieftains, Shah Abbas followed the example of Shah Tahmasb by forming a regiment in the army to subdue the Qizilbash forces. This new regiment consisted of Georgian, Armenian, and Cherkissian slaves, who had converted to Islam.

Shah Abbas temporarily settled the problem of the Ottomans through signing a peace treaty. This allowed him to turn his attention to the Uzbeks.

1590 Shah Abbas decided to relocate his capital from the insecure borderlands to Isfahan, the center of the country.

1590 Naqsh-e Jahan Royal Square was founded in Isfahan by Shah Abbas.

This 8 hectare (20 acre) square is an elongated rectangle which covered a space far larger than the contemporary European plazas. The royal square, primarily for state ceremonies and sports, was conceived, designed and constructed in about 5 years,

1590 The most significant part of the urban program carried out by Shah Abbas in his new capital was the relocation of the commercial, religious, and political center of the city southwest toward the Zayandeh river.

1595 A two-kilometer-long (1.3 miles) bazaar connected the square near the old Jame' mosque to the new one at Naqsh-e Jahan.

1596 The construction of the Ali Qapu ("Sublime Porte") Palace on the west side of the square began.

The structure was originally planned to be an entranceway to the royal gardens. However, it was repeatedly modified and extended upwards in the following sixty years as it developed into an audience hall. The interior was superbly decorated with fantastic plaster vaults suspended from the ceiling, and pierced in the shapes of the Chinese porcelains and Persian lusterwares, which is said to have had a marvelous acoustic effect. The interior is covered with murals, all rendered in delicate polychrome relief. Many small rooms for private entertainment have fireplaces and are open on one side.

1596 A complex of a large caravanserai, a small mosque and an unusually large bath house were built in Kerman (1596-1606) by Ganj Ali Khan, governor of the area under Shah Abbas.

1598 Shah Abbas defeated an Uzbek army led by Din Mohammad Khan.

He signed an agreement with local tribes, and secured the Northeast against further attacks.

1598 Shah Abbas officially moved his capital from Qazvin to Isfahan.

1600 Chahar Bagh ("Quarter Garden") Avenue, the other great feature of Shah Abbas' city plan, was constructed in Isfahan.

It was to provide a main road of unprecedented width and splendor through the heart of the new city, of which it would be the axis. The palace grounds provided the link between the square and the Chahar Bagh. The avenue was lined with ministers' palaces on each side separated by open arcades ensuring that the gardens would be plainly visible. It was planted with eight rows of planes and poplars, with rose hedges and jasmine bushes between them. The water channels, which ran the whole length of the avenue down to the river, were faced with onyx.

1601 **The shrine of Imam Reza (A) was renovated and extended under the patronage of Shah Abbas.**

1602 **Shah Abbas drove the Portuguese from Bahrain.**
After 80 years of unrest, the Persians took Bahrain and secured it against assaults by the Portuguese and Omanis. Shah Abbas then decided to put an end to almost a century long Portuguese occupation of Hormuz.

1602 **The second phase of construction of the royal square in Isfahan began.**
Shops were developed around the perimeter and let at low rents to attract merchants from the old city center.

1602 **Allahverdi Khan Bridge, or Si-o Seh Pol ("Bridge of thirty-three arches"), was erected at the southern end of the Chahar Bagh boulevard.**
It was to link Isfahan on the north bank of the Zayandeh river with the prospective Armenian quarter of New Julfa on the south bank.

1602 **The mosque of Sheikh Lutfullah was founded on the east side of the Square.**
The mosque has a familiar square base, squinch zone form of the dome-chamber, but it is not of a typical four-ivan type. The interior of this mosque is the most perfectly balanced space in Safavid architecture. The construction continued until 1619.

<u>1603</u> Shah Abbas set out to reclaim the land he had submitted to the Ottomans.

<u>1603</u> Queen Elizabeth of England and Ireland (b.1558), whose reign is considered one of the greatest periods of English history, died.

____ Having secured Tabriz, which had almost been taken by the Ottomans, Shah Abbas successfully attacked Naxcivan and Erivan.

<u>1604</u> He transplanted a major part of the population of Armenian Julfa to Isfahan—to a place they called New Julfa.

Shah Abbas depopulated eastern Armenia to create an empty tract between Persia and the Ottomans.

<u>1605</u> Persian troops led by Commander Allahverdi Khan defeated the Ottomans near Lake Van.

____ Shortly afterwards, the Ottomans launched their counterattack which was crushed near Tabriz.

____ Shah Abbas delivered the final blow against the Ottomans, demonstrating his military talent and supremacy.

<u>1607</u> The last areas held by the Ottomans after the Amasiyyeh peace treaty were retaken.

<u>1612</u> Work began on the Royal Mosque in Isfahan, located on the south side of the meidan.

This magnificent mosque follows the typical four-ivan plan of a central court surrounded by arcades, with an ivan in the middle of each of the four sides and a domed sanctuary beyond the ivan on the Qibla side. The construction of this monumental mosque was not finished until 1630, a year after Shah Abbas' death.

<u>1613</u> Commander Allahverdi Khan died.

The former Georgian slave rose to the ranks of commander of the slave army, governor of Fars province, and commander of the Persian army.

<u>1615</u> Shah Abbas drove the Portuguese from Port of Gamberon.

Port of Gamberon was named Bandar Abbas ("Port of Abbas") to commemorate this military triumph.

____ The English East India Company made an approach to the court of Isfahan to sell woolen textiles and buy Persian silks.

1616 William Shakespeare, the outstanding English playwright and poet, died.

1617 The first English agency was opened in Shiraz.

1618 Shah Abbas granted the English a monopoly to export Persian silks.

1619 Shah Abbas permitted the English to open another trading station at Jask Island in the Persian Gulf.

____ Shah Abbas drove the Portuguese from Ra's ul-Khaima, now in the UAE, and out of all Persian waters.

1621 English ships participated in the Persian expedition against the Portuguese to liberate Hormuz.

____ Shah Abbas granted the customs franchise of the port of Bandar Abbas to the English Company.

1622 Sheikh Baha'i, a major figure in the cultural revival of Safavid Persia under Shah Abbas, died at 76.

In his poetry, Sheikh Baha'i expounded complex mystical doctrines in simple and unadorned verse. His best-known poem, 'Nan-o halva' ("Bread and Sweets"), describes the experiences of an itinerant holy man, who may well be Sheikh Baha'i himself, on the Mecca pilgrimage. 'Kashkul' ("The Beggar's Bowl"), containing both stories and verses, was translated widely. His major work of astronomy is 'Tashrih ul-aflak' ("Anatomy of the Heavens"). Sheikh Baha'i was responsible for the revival of mathematical sciences in Persia, the study of which had been neglected for more than 100 years. His 'Khulasat ul-hisab' ("The Essentials of Arithmetic"), written in Arabic, was translated several times into Persian and German. The work was a standard textbook until the beginning of the 20th century.

____ English supremacy was established in the Persian Gulf.

1624 Shah Abbas recaptured Baghdad and areas to the North including Kirkuk, Mosul and Shahruz from the Ottomans.

1629 Shah Abbas the Great died, and Crown Prince Safi ascended the Safavid throne.

1630 The invading Ottoman army suffered defeats in various areas.
These areas included Hamadan and Baghdad, leaving many hundred Ottomans captive. Shah Safi released two thousand Ottoman captives.

1630 Johannes Kepler (b.1571), German astronomer, died.
He explained the motion of the planets round the sun and is regarded as one of the founders of modern astronomy.

1632 The Ottomans were again defeated near Lake Van.

1634 Erivan was taken by the Ottomans, but Shah Safi soon recaptured it.

1635 Reza Abbasi, the major Persian painter of the Isfahan school and the favourite painter of Shah Abbas the Great, died at 65 in Isfahan.
Reza was the last great Persian painter of originality.
His style had an everlasting influence on the Isfahan school (1597-1722).

1636 Uzbeks were defeated in several battles by Shah Safi.

1637 Having retaken Baghdad, the Ottomans pressed for peace.

1639 A peace treaty was signed between the Persians and Ottomans.

1640 Fendereski, Persian scholar and philosopher, died.
He was respected by both the Safavid Shah Abbas and the Mughal court in India.

1640 Molla Sadra, the foremost representative of the Illuminationist, or Ishraqi, school of philosopher-mystics, died in Basra on a pilgrimage to Mecca.
He produced several works, the most famous of which was his 'Asfar' ("Journeys"). He is commonly regarded by Persians as the greatest philosopher Persia has produced.

1642 Shah Safi died.

1642 Ten-year-old Prince Abbas ascended the Safavid throne as Shah Abbas II.

1642 Galileo Galilei (b.1564), Italian astronomer, physicist and one of the founders of modern science, died.

1643 Chehel Sotun ("Forty Columns") Palace was reconstructed.
Chehel Sotun was the Palace where Shah Abbas II received the credentials of ambassadors and foreign delegations.

1644 Ali Qapu Palace was embellished by the order of the Shah.

1647 Construction work on Khaju Bridge, begun in 1642 on the foundations of a fifteenth-century span in Isfahan, resumed.

1647 Chehel Sotun Palace was founded in Isfahan.
The palace was intended for official receptions and audiences.

1649 Shah Abbas II took Kandahar from the Mughal ruler, Shah Jahan.

1650 The Portuguese faced a final defeat in the Persian Gulf.

1650 Khaju bridge was inaugurated.
It lay astride the old road to Shiraz and linked the Khaju quarter due south of the meidan with the Zoroastrian quarter on the south bank. In the center is a raised octagonal pavilion, from where the ruler was able to enjoy the spectacles staged on the river below.

1659 Molla Mohammad Taqi Majlesi (b.1594), a prominent Shia religious leader and author, died.
He was the father of Molla Mohammad Baqir Majlesi, another influential cleric of the Safavid court.

1666 According to Chardin, the French traveler, Isfahan had 162 mosques, 48 madrasas, 182 caravanserais and 273 bathhouses.

1666 The Great Fire of London took place.

1667 Shah Abbas II died at 35.
During the successful twenty five years of his reign, Shah Abbas II and his wise minister, Khalifeh Sultan, faced little internal crisis. Despite frequent attempts by the Russians, Georgia remained part of Persia.

1667 Prince Soleiman (Shah Safi II) became king of Persia.

Tavernier, the French traveler, witnessed Shah Soleiman's coronation.

1669 Hasht Behesht ("Eight Paradises") Palace was erected in Isfahan under Shah Soleiman.
This is a two-storey square pavilion in the Bagh-e Bolbol ("Garden of the Nightingale"). The building is composed of four blocks of rooms each with two storeys arranged around a central space. Its name refers to a type of palace known since the fifteenth century in Herat and Tabriz.

1669 Dutch painter Rembrandt (b.1606), one of the greatest portrait painters of all time, died.

1675 Turkmen invasion of northeast was crushed.
The cities of Astarabad, Damghan and Semnan remained parts of Persia.

1677 Sa'eb Tabrizi (b.1603), Persian poet, died.
He was one of the most prolific poets of his time, and is highly praised by Oriental critics.

1679 Molla Mohsen Feiz Kashani (b.1598), one of the greatest scholars of Safavid Persia, died.
He wrote on tradition, philosophy, theoretical Sufism, ethics, and jurisprudence, and composed commentaries on the Qur'an, poetry and prayers.

1694 Shah Soleiman died.
Shah Soleiman was probably the least competent of the Safavid kings. He ruled for twenty eight years on the merits of his vizier.

1694 Prince Hossein became king of Persia.

1698 Molla Mohammad Baqir Majlesi (b.1627), an authoritative jurist, a most prolific collector of traditions, and an influential author of the Twelver Shi'ism, died.

1712 Mahmud the Afghan occupied Kerman.

1722 Prince Tahmasb went to Qazvin to assemble troops to fight the Afghans.

1722 A complex of buildings, begun in 1694, including a madrasa, known as the Madar-e Shah ("mother of the

Shah"), as well as a caravanserai, stables, and a bazaar was completed on Chahar Bagh Avenue.

This is perhaps the last architectural achievement from the Safavid period. The complex represents a return to the grandiose planning favored by Shah Abbas I.

1722 Shah Sultan Hossein was deposed by invading Afghans.

Shah Sultan Hossein handed the Persian Crown over to Mahmud the Afghan who ascended the throne two days later at Chehel Sotun Palace.

1723 Prince Tahmasb proclaimed himself Shah Tahmasb II in Qazvin.

1724 Mahmud the Afghan was killed by his cousin, Ashraf the Afghan, who claimed the Persian throne as his successor.

1726 Ashraf the Afghan signed a peace treaty with the Ottoman Emperor recognizing him as 'Amir al-Mu'minin'.

'Amir al-Mu'minin' is a title which means the Commander of the Faithful, or the Supreme Islamic Ruler.

1726 Fighting alongside Qajar troops, Commander Nadir defeated Mahmud Sistani, the governor of Khorasan, and occupied Mashad in the name of Shah Tahmasb II.

1727 Sir Isaac Newton (b.1642), English mathematician and physicist, died. His description of the laws of mechanics and gravitation, with its concept of force and mass, was the greatest contribution to physics until the work of Einstein.

1729 Commander Nadir defeated Ashraf the Afghan near Damghan.

He was forced to retreat to Tehran area where he managed to reorganize his troops aided by Ottoman artillery, and headed for Isfahan.

1729 Commander Nadir defeated Ashraf the Afghan for the second time near Isfahan.

____ Nadir entered Isfahan, followed three days later by Shah Tahmasb II.

____ Forty days later Nadir crushed Ashraf for the last time near Shiraz.

Following his decisive defeat, Ashraf fled before Nadir and was killed in Beluchistan, bringing to an end the brief Afghan adventure in Persia.

1732 Shah Tahmasb II was forced to abdicate in favor of his infant son, who was to rule as Shah Abbas III.

1733 Nadir's forces ended Ottoman occupation by killing their Commander, Othman Pasha.

1734 Nadir ended the Ottoman-Russian occupation of Darband, Baku, Erivan, and subdued other areas in the Caucasus.

1736 Persians and Russians signed a pact against the Ottomans.

Following his great victories, Nadir assembled all the senior officials and expressed his intention to retire to his homeland. Reminding the members that both Shah Tahmasb II and Shah Abbas III were alive, he called on the assembly to appoint the king. The assembly acclaimed his heroism, and appointed him as king of Persia.

Afsharid and Zand Period

1736 – 1795

Having utterly defeated the Afghans in a series of brilliant victories, Nadir first restored the Safavids back to the Persian throne. But when they proved incompetent, he deposed them and established the Afsharid dynasty, named after the Turkish tribe to which he belonged. His most notable victory among several successful military campaigns was over the Mughal Empire of India after which he returned home with vast amounts of loot, including the fabulous Peacock Throne and the Koh-i-noor diamond. His empire at its height rivaled the territorial extent of the ancient Persian empires. Although brilliantly successful as a soldier and general, Nadir Shah was harsh and ruthless and these traits became more pronounced as he grew older. The consequence was that revolt after revolt against him occurred. In the end, he was assassinated by his own troops. Following the death of Nadir Shah, Karim Khan Zand consolidated his power as the ruler of southern Iran and founded the Zand dynasty. During his years of power, he gave the areas under his control a much-needed peace from continual warfare. He encouraged agriculture and commerce.

1736 Commander Nadir was proclaimed king of Persia.

1738 Having reunited Persia, Nadir Shah carried the arms of the nation to Kandahar while his son, Reza Qoli Mirza, conquered Balkh, Ghondooz and Badakhshan.

1739 Nadir Shah marched from Afghanistan into India.

Having crossed the Indus and taken the city of Lahore, Nadir defeated the Indian army of 300,000 men and 2,000 elephants. After a two-month stay in Delhi, Nadir reinstated Mohammad Shah as the Emperor of most of India, but compelled him to pay an enormous indemnity, including the famous gem-studded Peacock Throne of Emperor Shah Jahan.

1746 Nadir Shah one more time crushed the Ottomans headed by Yakon Pasha.

Yakon Pasha and 12,000 Ottomans were killed in the war, and some 5,000 were taken prisoner.

1747 A peace treaty was signed by the Persians and the Turks.

According to the treaty, the borders established by Shah Safi and Sultan Murad II in 1639 were recognized, right of passage and freedom of travel for Persian pilgrims was granted, ambassadors were exchanged, and bilateral custom duties were devised.

1747 Having ruled for eleven years, Nadir was assassinated while campaigning against a revolt by his Cossack Generals.

1747 Ali Qoli Khan, Nadir's nephew, began to rule as Ali Shah.

____ Ebrahim Khan, Ali Shah's brother, called himself Ebrahim Shah in Isfahan, and defeated Ali Shah in a battle near Zanjan.

1748 Shahrokh, Nadir's nephew in Mashad, declared himself king.

____ Ebrahim Shah was defeated and blinded by the supporters of Shahrokh in Qom.

____ Ali Shah was killed in Mashad.

1749 Mohammad Motavali, the governor of Mashad, arrested and blinded Shahrokh, and called himself Shah Soleiman II.

____ Forty days later he was deposed by Shahrokh's supporters, and Shahrokh took over again.

____ Karim Khan, belonging to a Lur tribe that had been transplanted from Malayer to Daregaz region in Khorasan by Nadir Shah, was leading his tribe back to its homeland.

1751 Ali Mardan Khan, leader of Bakhtiari tribe, was assassinated.

1751 Karim Khan Zand became leader and made Shiraz his capital.

1757 Mohammad Hassan Khan Qajar was killed by another Qajar from a different family while fleeing before Karim Khan's men.

1759 Karim Khan ended the long struggle with the Qajars.

1761 After four years of hiding, the son of Mohammad Hassan Khan, Agha Mohammad Khan, was castrated and taken hostage at the court of Karim Khan Zand in Shiraz.
Agha Mohammad Khan later deposed the last of the Zands and founded the Qajar dynasty.

1763 Karim Khan gave the East India Company rights to establish a factory in Bushehr.
The factory soon became a center of commercial activity that led to the eventual predominance of the British in southern Persia.

1766 Karim Khan glorified his capital city of Shiraz.
His contributions include broad avenues and more than 25 public buildings, a mosque, a bazaar, and a palace.
The most important were grouped around a meidan, following the arrangement introduced by Safavids in Isfahan and Kerman. Most of these buildings are decorated with patterned stone dados and tiles painted with naturalistic flowers in distinctive rose and yellow tones. The Vakil complex included a bath house and a vaulted bazaar to its east.

1773 Shiraz's new Jame' Mosque of Vakil was inaugurated.

1775 The Fight for American independence from Britain started and continued until 1783.

1776 Karim Khan's troops attacked the Turks and reclaimed the occupied Basra.

1779 Karim Khan Zand died at 80.

Karim Khan was a courageous and benevolent but modest man who never assumed the title of "Shah" and ruled for thirty one years 'Vakil' ("Regent of People"). He gave the country a period of much-needed peace.

____ Family disputes over Karim Khan's legacy followed his death.

____ Five of Karim Khan's family sat on the throne in succession until the throne fell to Lotf Ali Khan.

1783 Georgia renounced all connections with Persia and signed a treaty with Russia.

1783 Ahmad Ibn al-Khalifa drove the Persians out of Bahrain.

His family has ruled in Bahrain ever since.

1784 The British government introduced legislation to bring the East India Company under its political control.

The Company was to act as an undisguised instrument of British colonial policy.

____ Empress Catherine of Russia enjoined the race for the domination of Asia.

Russia looked at Persia as an area of economic exploitation and strategic possibilities.

1785 Agha Mohammad Khan, who had escaped from the court of Zands to his tribal country in the north after Karim Khan's death, gathered a large force and embarked upon a war of conquest.

1788 Shiraz was besieged by Agha Mohammad Khan.

1789 The youthful and magnanimous Lotf Ali Khan, second cousin of Karim Khan Zand, ascended the throne.

He was a great military commander, but not so much a political ruler. During his short reign, he confronted more challenges than most of his predecessors. He left Shiraz to gather more troops to fight against Agha Mohammad Khan. He found himself betrayed upon his return to Shiraz, but put down the insurrection.

1789 The French Revolution took place.

1789 Leaving Ebrahim Khan in charge of his capital, Lotf Ali Khan left Shiraz to pursue Agha Mohammad Khan.

Lotf Ali Khan found himself betrayed again near Isfahan, and was compelled to return to the capital Shiraz, where he was barred entry.

1789 George Washington (1723-1799), American soldier and statesman, became the first president of the USA; he led the new nation until 1797.

1790 Lotf Ali Khan entered the port of Bushehr to re-organize his forces.

1791 Agha Mohammad Khan defeated Lotf Ali Khan Zand.

Lotf Ali Khan almost managed to defeat the Qajar forces, but nightfall allowed the Qajars to re-assemble, and Lotf Ali Khan chose to retreat.

1792 Ibn Abdul Wahhab (b.1703 in Arabia), a Hanbalite theologian from Najd and the founder of Wahhabism, died.

1793 Having fought the Qajars for two years, Lotf Ali Khan finally decided to take refuge in Kerman.

After a four-month siege, Kerman fell to Agha Mohammad Khan at the cost of many hundreds of people slaughtered and thousands blinded. Lotf Ali Khan fled to Bam, where he was finally arrested and handed over to Agha Mohammad Khan.

1794 Lotf Ali Khan Khan was executed in Tehran.

1795 Agha Mohammad Khan marched to restore Persian power over Georgia, and captured Tiflis and Erivan.

Qajar Period

1795 – 1925

Following the death of Karim Khan Zand, Agha Mohammad Khan, a leader of the Turkmen Qajar tribe, managed to eliminate all his rivals and to reunify Iran under a new dynasty. The Qajars attempted to assert Iran's sovereignty over Georgia and the Caucasus but were disastrously defeated by Russia in two wars and thus lost all those territories. This led to Russian commercial and consular agents' entrance to Iran, and began a diplomatic rivalry between Russia and Britain that victimized Iran. During the Qajar rule western science, technology, and educational methods were introduced, and the country's modernization was begun. Under popular pressure, first constitution that called for some curtailment of monarchial power was granted towards the end of this period.

1796 Agha Mohammad Khan was proclaimed Shah of Persia.
He established Tehran as the capital of the country.
He reaffirmed the Shia faith as the state religion.

1797 Agha Mohammad Khan was assassinated, and his nephew, Fath Ali, ascended the throne.
Fath Ali was unequal to the challenges of internal and external crisis.

1799 The first British mission from Bombay came to the court of Fath Ali Shah to convince him that his safety lay in alliance with the British.

1800 Hassan Ali Mahallati, the future Aqa Khan and the leader of the Nizari Ismailis, was born in Persia.

1800 Russia annexed Georgia in their first attack.

____ The second British mission under Captain Malcolm ended in a treaty whereby Fath Ali Shah agreed not to make peace with the Afghans.

____ Britain agreed to assist Persia militarily against the Afghans or French.
The British successfully made Afghanistan into a buffer state between Persia and India.

____ The East India Company gained more commercial privileges and tax exemptions in Persia.

1804 Napoleon (b.1769) became Emperor of France and ruled for ten years. As Emperor, he conquered most of Europe, failing only in his attempts on Russia and Britain.

1804 The French offered Persia an alliance against Russia.

1804 Persia was driven to enter war with Russia.

____ Prince Abbas Mirza, a great patriot and courageous military commander, led the Persian forces in the first Russian imposed war.

____ At his side, Abbas Mirza had Qa'em Magham Farahani, the most notable politician and administrator of his time.

____ Qa'em Magham Farahani realized the urgent need to carry out internal reforms in all fields of public life, spiritual, political, military, and literary.

1806 The French sought to finalize an alliance with Persia through a special ambassador.
Having waited for four years and failed to obtain the promised assistance from the British, Fath Ali Shah turned to the French.

1807 Mirza Taqi, the future Prime Minister Amir Kabir, was born at Farahan.

1807 Persia and France signed the treaty of Finkenstein.
The treaty aimed to provide for mutual aid against Russia and Britain.

1809 Sir Hartford Jones signed a preliminary treaty with Persia by which England promised military and financial aid to Persia.

1811 The 1809 treaty was ratified by London.

1812 The first lithographic press was established in Tabriz by Qa'em Magham Farahani.

1813 Russia attacked Persia.

1813 Abbas Mirza led the forces under his command into battle in the second imposed war with Russia, but he was unsuccessful.
The 1809 treaty proved worthless.

1813 Fath Ali Shah was compelled to sign the vaguely worded treaty of Golestan with Russia.
This was ironically made possible through the influence of the British representative, Sir Gore Ouseley.
The Golestan treaty marked the beginning of Russian influence at Qajar courts.

1813 Persia had to abandon all rights to Georgia including the right to maintain a navy in the Caspian waters.

1813 Persia ceded the northern territories and the Persian navy was exiled from the Caspian.

1813 The Russians set up a Legation in Tehran.

1814 A definitive treaty was signed with Britain.

1819 James Watt (b.1739), Scottish inventor who developed the design of the steam-engine, died.

1826 Hostilities with Russia broke out, and Persia was forced to sign the horrendous treaty of Turkamanchai.
Persia surrendered all the northern territory of the Aras River, paid a heavy indemnity to Russia, and granted extra-territorial privileges to Russian citizens.
The Turkamanchai treaty was to be taken by Europeans as a model for treatment of Persia in later years.

1827 Ludvig Van Beethoven (b.1770), German composer, died.
His music represents for many the supreme example of the late classical period and the beginning of Romanticism.

1829 Haji Molla Ahmad Naraqhi (b.1771), Shia religious leader, man of letters, social critic and religious polemicist, died.
Despite his friendly relations with the Qajar Fath Ali Shah, he refused to recognize the legitimacy of his rule, maintaining that only qualified jurists carry the authority of the Hidden Imam. This line of argument provided an important source of reasoning for Ayatollah Khomeini (R).

1829 Amir Kabir joined a diplomatic team and was sent to Russia.
He was sent together with a handful of court officials to St Petersburg and the Russian Caucasus, where they visited schools, factories, chambers of commerce and theatres.

____ Fath Ali Shah honored the leader of the Ismaili community with the title of Aqa Khan.

1831 George Wilhelm Friedrich Hegel (b.1770), German philosopher, died. He saw human history as the development of the idea of freedom.

1832 Johann Wolfgang Goethe (b.1749), German writer, died. He is most famous as a founder of German national literature through poems, plays, and novels.

1833 Abbas Mirza died at 44.
For many years he was the governor-general of Azerbaijan. He was known for his bravery, generosity, and devotion to military art.

1834 Fath Ali Shah, who had waged five uneven wars in his lifetime died, and Mohammad Shah succeeded him.

1836 Aqa Khan rebelled against the central Qajar government.

1837 Amir Kabir returned to the Caucasus and spent four years in Erzincan, eastern Turkey, as an official negotiator drawing up the Persian-Ottoman frontier.

1838 Russian expansion began with the First Expedition to Khiva.

____ Persia's traditional society was becoming a defenseless victim of Western pressure.

1840 Aqa Khan fled to Sind.

Owing to the religious intolerance, the Ismaili Community left for India. Aqa Khan later acquired great wealth in Bombay.

1844 Babism was founded by the Bab Seyyed Ali Mohammad of Shiraz.

1847 Amir Kabir returned to Tehran and was appointed as the tutor to the Crown Prince Nassereddin, and then was promoted Chief Army Minister.

1848 Nassereddin became Shah of Persia.

1848 Mirza Taqi Khan Amir Kabir, who had begun as a protégé of Qa'em Magham Farahani, became the Prime Minister.

Having paid huge war indemnity to Russia as part of the Treaty of Turkamanchai of 1826, Persia was virtually bankrupt, central government was weak, and most provinces were autonomous.

During the next two and a half years, Amir Kabir initiated important reforms in virtually all sectors of society.

Government expenditure was slashed, and a distinction was made between the privy and public purses. The instruments of central administration were overhauled.

Foreign interference in Persia's domestic affairs was reduced, and foreign trade was encouraged. Public works such as the bazaar in Tehran were undertaken.

Amir Kabir issued a decree banning elaborate and excessively formal writing in government documents, and thus initiated a modern Persian prose style.

____ Amir Kabir established a secular Western-style college of technology, Dar ol-Fonun, in Tehran for training a new cadre of administrators.

1849 Russian armies gradually advanced to Aral Sea.
British rule over the entire sub-continent of India was almost complete.

1851 Extensive reforms antagonized various politicians who had been excluded from the government.
They regarded Amir Kabir as a threat to their interests, and formed a coalition against him, in which the queen mother was active. She convinced the young Shah that Amir Kabir wanted to take over the throne.

1851 Amir Kabir, a victim of intrigues and plots among those who opposed his reforms, was dismissed from his duties by the order of the Shah, and was exiled to Kashan.

1852 Amir Kabir, the most prominent reformist statesman of the time, was murdered on Shah's orders at Fin Garden in Kashan.
During the short period of his Premiership, he took part in diplomatic missions to Russia and Turkey, made strenuous efforts to introduce modernising measures, and established the basis for modern Persian nationalism.

1859 Yaghma Jandaqhi (b.1782), Persian poet, died.

1860 The Masonic cult 'Free Masons' was introduced in Persia.

1861 Abraham Lincoln (b.1809), became the 16th president of America. Supporting the policy to end slavery in America, he issued a proclamation freeing all slaves. Later, the Congress amended the Constitution to end slavery. He was assassinated in 1865.

1861 The four-year American Civil War started. This was a war between the federal government and 11 Southern states that asserted their right to secede from the Union.

1864 Sheikh Morteza Ansari (b.1799), Shia mujtahed, died.
His widely recognized religious leadership in the Shia world had not been surpassed.

____ Since Persia did not possess adequate military strength to throw back the Europeans, some Persians propagated the adherence to the concept of pan-Islamism, the unity of all Muslim nations. Pan-Islamism was not limited to Persia; it spread to certain other Muslim countries, including Muslim India.

1864 The first telegraph line of Persia was laid.

1865 A girls school was founded in Tehran.

1868 The Amir of Bukhara was defeated by the Russians.

1869 Suez Canal was opened.

1870 A network of Indo-European telegraph lines was built.

1870 Charles Huffham Dickens (b.1812), English novelist, died.

1872 Nassereddin Shah granted several extraordinary economic concessions to Baron Reuter.

Reuter acquired rights to build railways, work mines, and set up a state bank in return for completely hypothetical benefits for the Persian government.

1873 Khiva was conquered by the Russians.

1878 Nassereddin Shah employed Austrians to build up a modern army for Persia.

1878 Reza Savadkuhi, the future Reza Khan Mirpanj and the founder the Pahlavi dynasty, was born to an army officer in the Savadkuh region of Mazandaran.

1878 Akhundzadeh (b.1811), the first writer of original plays in Azeri Turkish, died.

1878 Haji Hadi Sabzevari (b.1797), philosopher and poet, died.

He disseminated and clarified the doctrines of Molla Sadra Shirazi. Nassereddin Shah ordered a mausoleum to be built for him in Mashad.

1879 A Persian Cossack Brigade, a force of 1,500 men, was created on the Russian model.

1881 Aqa Khan died. Aqa Khan II Ali Shah became the ruler of Nizari Ismaili community.

1881 Russian armies defeated the Turkmans, and the Czarist empire began to loom heavily over Persia.

Persia now lay helpless between the British and Russian empires.

1882 Charles Robert Darwin (b.1809), British naturalist, died. He developed the theory of evolution by natural selection.

1882 Giuseppe Garibaldi (b.1807), Italian military leader, died. He played an important part in the struggle for a united and independent Italy.

1885 Aqa Khan II was followed by Aqa Khan III.

1885 Victor Marie Hugo (b.1802), French novelist, poet and playwright, died. He was one of the leading figures in the Romantic movement in France. His best-known novels are Notre Dame de Paris and Les Miserables.

1890 A British company received concessions for the production, sale and export of all tobacco.

This became a landmark in a movement toward Persia's political revival.

1890 Vincent Van Gogh (b.1853), Dutch artist, died.

____ The celebrated cleric Mirza Shirazi issued a 'Fitwa' ("Religious Decree") prohibiting Tobacco.

____ People responded to the Fitwa by boycotting tobacco at a nationwide scale.

This became known as the Tobacco Movement.

1892 Nassereddin Shah was compelled to cancel the tobacco right.

He had to pay a compensation of half a million pounds sterling, borrowed from Reuter's Imperial Bank, which in turn marked the beginning of the Persian national debt.

1892 In answer to a call from the clergy for resistance, Seyyed Jamaleddin Assad Abadi played an important part in stimulating popular indignation over the actions of the Shah.

1892 Baha'ollah (b.1817 in Tehran), founder of the Baha'i faith, died in Acre, Palestine.

He was one of the first disciples of the Bab Seyyed Ali Mohammad of Shiraz. In 1867, in Edirne, Western Turkey, he publicly declared himself to be the divinely chosen Imam-Mahdi ('Rightly Guided Leader'), whom the Bab had foretold. In 1868, he was banished to Acre, where he wrote the 'Most Holy Book', the fundamental work of his religion.

1892 Reza Khan joined the Cossack Brigade at the age of fourteen.

1895 Louis Pasteur (b.1822), French bacteriologist, died. He discovered the role of micro-organisms in fermentation and disease.

1895 Seyyed Mirza Khansari (b.1811), Persian religious scholar and writer, died.

He is best known for his biographical dictionary, which has enjoyed a great reputation.

1896 The Olympic Games were revived by Baron Pierre de Coubertin (b.1863 in Paris).

The first modern Olympic Games were held in Athens.

1896 Nassereddin Shah was assassinated by a pan-Islamist, Mirza Reza Kermani.

1896 Prince Mozaffareddin became Shah of Persia.

1897 Jamaleddin Assad Abadi (b.1838 at Asad Abad, Persia), philosopher, writer, orator and journalist, died in Istanbul.

He is known as the founder of modern Muslim anti-colonialism. With him began the reform movement which gave rise to the 'Salafiyyeh' and later, the 'Muslim Brothers'. He preached the necessity of a Muslim revival. His ultimate objective was to unite Muslim states including Shia Persia into a single Caliphate. The Pan-Islamic idea was the great passion of his life.

1898 Several telegraph lines, managed by Persian government and laid by English and German firms, crossed the country linking India, Europe, Russia and Great Britain.

1900 At the turn of the century, Persia had a population of less than ten million.

Ninety percent lived by farming and herding.

More than fifty percent were peasants.

About twenty five percent belonged to nomadic tribes.
Less than twenty percent lived in towns.
Tehran, the capital city, had a population of 200,000.
Tabriz, the second largest city, had just under 200,000.
Isfahan, the third largest city, had about 100,000.

1900 **Ruhollah Musavi Khomeini (R), who was to lead the Islamic revolution of 1979 was born in Khomein, western Persia.**
He was the son and grandson of the Shia religious leaders of his area. When he was five months old his father was killed on the orders of a local landlord.

1900 Friedrich Nietzsche (b.1844), German philosopher, died. His concept of a 'superman', superior to the rest of humanity and to Christian morality, influenced the ideas of Nazism.

1901 Queen Victoria of the United Kingdom (b.1819) died. She was a powerful symbol of Britain at the height of its empire.

1901 **Mozaffareddin Shah agreed to a tariff preference to Russia and rights in oil excavation to Britain.**
He had learnt little from the experiences of his predecessors.

1901 **The D'Arcy Oil Concession was granted.**
The three factors that led to the grant of this oil concession to a British company were Qajar ignorance, personal interest and disregard of national will. The glorious edifice of what was to become a multi-million dollar company was in fact founded on this tripod.

____ **Popular demand for a national constitution arose.**
Having realized the potential strength of the Constitutionalists, the British authorities began to give moral and material aid to their movement.

1902 Abd ur-Rahman al-Kawakibi (b.1849 in Syria), pioneer in the theory of Pan-Arabism, died. In 1878 he had brought out the first Arabic weekly in his native town of Aleppo.

1905 **Two of the most prominent of the Olama of Tehran, Seyyed Abdollah Behbahani and Seyyed Mohammad Tabatabai,**

formed an alliance to mobilize support from among their theological students and urban masses.

1905 Years of protests against economic and territorial domination by Britain and Russia led to a revolution by clerics, merchants, and intellectuals forcing the weak Qajar Dynasty to accept the first constitution and parliament.

1905 Albert Einstein, German-born physicist, published his theory of relativity, which led to the equation $E=mc^2$, the basis of atomic energy.

1906 Constitutionalist leaders, mainly of Olama, served an ultimatum on the Shah to grant a constitution without delay, and demanded the dismissal of the Prime Minister, Ein od-Dowleh.

____ Mozaffareddin Shah retaliated by imprisoning a large number of the popular leaders.

The British Legation in Tehran became a sanctuary for those who escaped or were afraid of being arrested.

____ Ein od-Dowleh was compelled to resign.

____ Mozaffareddin Shah accepted the formation of a national assembly, the Majles.

The members of the assembly were to be elected for the first time to draw up a constitution which the Shah had to ratify.

Persia's first constitution or Fundamental Law was ready, and signed two months later by Mozaffareddin Shah.

1907 Mozaffareddin Shah died a few days after signing the Constitutional Law, and Crown Prince Mohammad Ali, the former governor of Azerbaijan, came to the Qajar throne.

____ Mohammad Ali Shah appointed Amin ol-Soltan as head of his government in April.

____ The new Shah attempted a coup to curb the Constitutionalist movement, which provoked public reaction.

____ Amin os-Soltan was assassinated on August 30.

Under the convention of London and St Petersburg, or the so-called Anglo-Russian Agreement, Persia was divided into rival spheres of influence, the North being reserved for Russia, South-East for Britain, and the central area constituting a neutral zone. Mohammad Ali Shah managed to retain his throne with his government left in the neutral area.

____ The Shah staged a second coup against the Constitutionalists with the assistance of the Cossack Brigade.

____ The Shah ordered Colonel Liakhov, Russian commander of the Cossack Brigade, to mount an artillery attack on the parliament building in Tehran whilst the Majles was in session.

Six regiments of the Brigade occupied Tehran, and a state of siege was declared. Liakhov was appointed Governor of the capital.

The Shah crushed the Assembly but he did not end the Constitutionalist movement.

____ Constitutionalists, led by the clergy in Najaf, Khorasan, and Mazandaran, retaliated swiftly and effectively by proclaiming a revolt, which soon reached Rasht and Isfahan.

____ Nationalist revolutionaries, led by the dominant figure Sattar Khan, were in control in Tabriz.

1908 Oil was excavated at Masjed Soleiman.

1908 Malkom Khan, Perso-Armenian diplomat, journalist and concession-monger, died.

He advocated governmental reform and systematic westernization and established the first Masonic lodge in Persia. In 1890 he embarked on the publication of a quite successful newspaper, 'The Law'.

____ Russian troops under the Czar Nicholas II entered Tabriz and another period of violence and cruelty began.

Tabriz had become the headquarters of the Constitutionalists who had taken up arms.

____ The re-grouped revolutionary forces marched towards Tehran, where they defeated the Cossack Brigade.

____ Mohammad Ali Shah fled as a refugee to the Russian Legation and then to Russia.

____ The Constitutionalists placed the eleven-year-old Crown Prince Ahmad on the throne.

____ The Czar demanded the Constitutionalists terminate the services of Morgan Shuster.

Shuster was a financial advisor whose mission was to re-organize Persian finances. Having acquired complete control over Persian finances, Shuster needed a competent military force under his control to collect taxes. He selected a British officer, Major C. B. Stokes, to command the new military force, the Treasury Gendarmerie. Russia refused to allow a British officer to command forces in Northern Persia. Shuster collided with Russia over the appointment of another Briton to serve in Northern Persia.

____ Tabriz was once again invaded, followed by another massacre of liberals and revolutionaries.

____ Holy Shrine of Imam Reza (A) in Mashad was bombarded.

1909 Two new anti-Shah movements began in Rasht and Isfahan, which led to a coalition of three forces from Tabriz, Rasht and Isfahan in Tehran.

1910 Count Lev Nikolaevich Tolstoy (b.1828), Russian writer, died.

His best known works are War and Peace (1869), an epic set at the time of Napoleon's invasion of Russia, and Anna Karenina.

1911 A Gendarmerie force was established by the pro-German Swedes to safeguard the roads of Persia.

1911 Two episodes effected a collision between Russia and the nationalists: the attempt by Mohammad Ali to recover his throne, and the mission of Morgan Shuster.

1911 Molla Akhund Khorasani (b.1839), distinguished Shia mojtahed from Tus in Persia, died.

Since 1906, his name had been associated with the Persian Constitutional Revolution as one of its most influential supporters.

1914 First World War broke out.

1914 The Russian troops were still in occupation of northern Persia.

____ Ottoman Empire entered the war which led to its destruction.

____ Persia declared neutrality in an attempt to avoid the storm.

____ The Ottomans attacked Azerbaijan.

____ The third Persian assembly met.

1915 The pro-German Swedish officers of the Gendarmerie were dismissed and Russian forces took over.

____ The Ottomans savagely massacred and mutilated hundreds of thousands of innocent Armenians.

____ Mirza Kuchak Khan became the leader of nationalist movement in Gilan.

____ The government of Mostowfi ol-Mamalek was forced to resign.

____ The government of Farman Farma was formed.

Farman Farma was a prominent pro-Entente politician. Entente meant alliance between France, Russia and Great Britain.

____ There was a considerable increase in German influence in Persia through the activities of German diplomats and agents.

Some of the better known German officers were Schunemann in Kermanshah, Pugin in Isfahan and Wilhelm Wassmuss in Fars. In Tehran the German Legation became a shelter for German and Austrian prisoners of war.

____ Third Persian Assembly disintegrated.

1916 The short lived Entente reached its peak of influence in Persia.

____ The government of Farman Farma was replaced by one headed by Sepahdar.

The British garrison in Iraq surrendered, releasing Ottoman forces for a new campaign into Persia.

The Ottomans invaded Western Persia and briefly controlled Kermanshah and Hamadan. Persia allowed the Entente powers to raise and control substantial Persian forces within their own spheres of influence. By this time the British sphere of influence had been extended to include the neutral zone. Russia and Britain gave financial help to Persia and returned the Customs to Persian control.

____ Sepahdar's government was brought down and one headed by Vosuq od-Dowleh was formed.

1917 The First Revolution of Russia made little difference for Persia.

____ The Ottoman advance was arrested and their forces were repulsed.

____ New secret opposition groups were organized to threaten Persian politicians who collaborated with Russia.

____ Vosuq's government was replaced by a new cabinet much less sympathetic to the Entente.

____ Elections for a fourth Assembly were announced.

____ The Second Russian Revolution resulted in the disintegration and evacuation of Russian troops from Northern Persia.

The Russian forces had effectively dominated Northern Persia since 1909.

1918 Samsaam os-Saltaneh formed a new cabinet.

1918 British women over 30 were allowed to vote for the first time.

1918 The new Soviet government formally renounced Czarist policies limiting Persian sovereignty.

Britain had to decide whether to pull out of Persia or to replace the Russians.

The Ottomans again attacked Azerbaijan, and the situation in Persia once more appeared to be critical.

Central Power collapsed, and that led to the establishment of British predominance in Persia.
British Foreign Secretary Lord Curzon supported the idea of a peaceful, stable, independent Persia.
British support was intended to create a nominally independent buffer state to protect British India and maintain British influence in the Middle East.

____ The pro-British cabinet of Vosuq od-Dowleh was formed.

1919 The compromising government of Vosuq od-Dowleh signed the new Anglo-Persian treaty with Lord Curzon, which provided for reorganization of Persian army and finances under British control and for construction of railways.

1919 Reza Khan was appointed a colonel in command of a regiment.

1920 Bolshevik forces landed in Gilan and gave their assistance to the movement for independence led by Mirza Kuchak Khan.

1920 Reza Khan Mirpanj was promoted Commander-in-Chief of the army.

1920 Sheikh Mohammad Khiabani (b.1879), Persian religious scholar and political leader from Azerbaijan, died.
He played a key role in the deposing of the Qajar Mohammad Ali Shah in 1909.

____ Persian ministers began to look at other possibilities for help from the United States and Soviet governments.

____ In order to preserve and maintain British influence in the South, Lord Curzon was compelled to abandon the North of Persia to Mirza Kuchak Khan and the Bolsheviks.

____ Seyyed Zia od-Din Tabatabai, a pro-British journalist, formed the next government.

1921 Reza Khan launched his vigorous three-year campaign for the territorial unification of Persia.

1921 Fourth Majles, dominated by the clerics, was elected.

1921 In Tehran, a group of moderate nationalists led by Seyyed Zia od-Din Tabatabai planned a coup.

1921 The military force of the coup was to be supplied by the Cossack Brigade then stationed in Qazvin under the command of Reza Khan.

1921 Reza Khan and Seyyed Zia od-Din Tabatabai met outside Tehran and made their plans.

1921 The next day Reza Khan occupied Tehran in an almost bloodless coup.

1921 Reza Khan seized power and helped to establish a strong central government backed by a national army.

Six weeks later Reza Khan was appointed Minister of War.

1921 Mirza Kuchak Khan, the eminent nationalist and reformist of Gilan, capitulated.

The coup was immediately followed by the rejection of the 1919 agreement with Britain, and acceptance of a proposed treaty of friendship with the Soviet Union according to which Russian troops left Persia and withdrew support for Mirza Kuchak Khan.

1922 Having been educated in various Islamic schools, Khomeini (R) moved to the holy city of Qom.

1922 Alexander Graham Bell (b.1847), Scottish scientist and inventor, died.

He is best known for having invented the telephone and the gramophone.

1923 Reza Khan, Minister of War since 1921, became Prime Minister.

1924 Nicolai Lenin (b.1870), Russian revolutionary leader, died.

After the overthrow of the Czar in 1917, he established control by the Bolshevik forces and became the leader of the new communist state.

1924 Reza Khan suppressed the tribal revolt of Sheikh Khaz'al, an independent chief who dealt with Anglo-Persian Oil Company.

1925 Ahmad Shah was deposed, and Qajar monarchy was ended by a resolution of the Majles assembly.

Pahlavi Period

1925 – 1975

Pahlavi dynasty takes its name from the language and script in use before Islam. Reza khan, the founder of the dynasty, was an Iranian army officer who rose through army ranks to become shah of Iran. During the years of power, the Pahlavis undertook the measure of radical reforms and rapid modernization. After the obligatory abdication of Reza Shah, popular and religious antagonism towards Mohammad Reza Shah intensified based upon his autocratic rule, forced westernization, and the activities of the secret police in suppressing dissent and opposition to his rule. This led to massive demonstrations, strikes, and civil unrest that eventually forced the departure of the Shah from the country and effected the establishment of an Islamic Republic.

1925 Reza Khan, a semiliterate military officer, proclaimed himself the first Shah of the new dynasty.

A ceremony was arranged in the Takieh Dowlat, attached to the royal palace, accommodating 3,000 courtiers, dignitaries, foreign diplomats, clerics, veterans and the press.

Reza Khan was aware that his will and determination would not change the whole landscape. His plans were to extend and strengthen the authority of central government, reconstruct the armed forces, and lay down the foundations of industrial development without putting his country in bond to foreign creditors.

____ For the first six years of his rule, Reza Shah established a close partnership with Teimurtash.

Mirza Abdul Hossein Khan Teimurtash, educated in Russia, was a politician of social grace, intelligence, energy, manners and charm who was to play a vital role in the assertion of Persian interests against the Soviet Union and the Europeans.

1925 200 trucks were imported to carry food stuffs from surplus to famine areas.

Ten years later 2,000 trucks and 1,000 motorcars were being imported every year.

1926 Reza Khan was crowned Reza Shah, and adopted 'Pahlavi' as the dynastic name.

1927 Reza Shah ended the capitulatory regime he had inherited from the Qajar dynasty.

1927 The Treaty of Guarantee and Neutrality was concluded with the Soviet Union.

The treaty secured mutual undertaking to refrain from aggression, and to remain neutral in the event of aggression by a third power; but it reiterated the right of the Soviet Union to send troops into Persia if a third party should use Persian territory against Russia.

1927 National Bank (Melli Bank) was formed to promote commerce and industry.

1927 A new Ministry of Justice was formed with Davar as Minister.

Davar, of middle-class origin, had graduated in law at the university of Geneva and was a young member of a group of progressive men who gathered around Reza Shah in the late twenties. A new civil code was enacted and new courts set up which effectively secularized the legal system and deprived the clergy of their exclusive judicial authority.

1930 Ruhollah Musavi (R) adopted the name of his home town, Khomein, as his surname.

1931 Trade agreements with the Soviet Union were renewed.

These agreements gave abnormal privileges to Russian trade delegations, and became a thin cover for espionage.

1931 Thomas Alva Edison (b.1847), American inventor, died.

1932 A treaty was signed between Persia and Turkey defining their shared frontier.

To pursue its national independence, Persia tried to seek strength by improving relations with neighboring powers, and to find a third outside power to balance Britain and Russia.

1933 Reza Shah accepted an invitation from Kemal Ataturk to visit Turkey.

1933 Teimurtash was dismissed by the Shah, and died soon afterwards, a broken man.

____ Reza Shah appointed Forughi as his first Prime Minister.

A former member of the Persian Peace Conference, Mohammad Ali Khan Forughi, the son of a university professor, earned a reputation for scholarship and honesty.

1934 Mirza Abol Qasim Aref (b.1880), Persian revolutionary poet and satirist, died.

His poetry is full of social satire, attacks on corruption, and nostalgia for Persia's great past.

1934 Reza Shah paid a state visit to Turkey.

He traveled to Ankara, where he was warmly received by Ataturk. This was the only state visit of his reign.

1934 A new agreement was reached on the frontier running along Arvand River, or Shatt al-Arab, dividing Iraq from Persia.

This agreement was reached over the crucial area right beside the Abadan refinery where Iraq had its only access to the sea.

1935 The First Academy (Farhangestan) was established and was active only until the abdication of Reza Shah Pahlavi in 1941.

1935 Reza Shah urged the world to refer to the country as Iran rather than Persia.

The land had for centuries been referred to by its inhabitants as 'Iran'. According to the best available information, the term 'Iran' was first used by Ardashir (224-240), the founder of Sassanian dynasty. Iran means the land of the 'Aryans', Indo-European nomadic peoples who, in several migrations, settled the land from the late second millennium BC. Iran is a more generic name for the greater territory embracing all ethnic groups, Persian and non-Persian, whereas Persia would only refer to the original homeland of the Persians, a province in the south of the country.

1935 Reza Shah's Queen appeared unveiled in public, leading to a forceful movement for the abolition of the veil.

1936 Sheikh Khaz'al (b.1860), died.

As the Sheikh of the area, he attempted to create an independent state in the oil-rich Iranian region of Mohammara, the present day Khorramshahr in southwestern province of Khuzestan. As the leader of the Muhasayn tribe, he also objected strongly to the proposal of the Iranian government to introduce Belgian customs officials into Khuzestan. He received support from the

British diplomatic mission in Tehran, but later lost it. His power was extinguished by Reza Khan Pahlavi in 1924.

1936 **Mohammad Mirza Na'ini (b.1860), prominent Shia religious leader, died.**
He was an active supporter of the Iranian constitutional revolution, and a noted constitutional ideologue. In his celebrated 'The Admonition and Refinement of the People', he argued that constitutionalism, despite its being a Western idea, was in harmony with Shi'ism.

1937 **Aqa Khan III, having acquired a leading position among the Muslims of India, became president of the League of Nations.**

1937 **Sheikh Abdol Karim Ha'eri (b.1859), Iranian religious leader, died.**
He argued that politics in the Muslim world were being controlled by Western powers and were consequently hostile to Islam. He trained many disciples who later on became religious leaders, the best known example being Ayatollah Khomeini (R).

1938 Mustafa Kemal Ataturk (b.1881), the founder and first President of the Turkish Republic (1923), died.
During his reign, he fiercely fought to modernize the country, to free it from foreign economic tutelage, and to secularize it.

1938 **Reza Shah and the Crown Prince went to Soltanabad and from there to Sefid Cheshmeh by train.**
Here the junction was established between the Caspian Sea and the Persian Gulf.

1938 Mohammad Iqbal Lahouri (b.1877), Indian philosopher and poet, died.
Able to write in English, Persian and Urdu, he taught the Muslims how to regain strength by developing their personality. He also insisted on the necessity of forming a separate Muslim state in Northwest India, which eventually was realized in the nation of Pakistan in 1947.

1939 Trans-Iranian railway, devised by Reza Shah, was completed.
1,400 km (870 miles) of railway with over 4,700 bridges and 224 tunnels together with 17,500 km (11,000 miles) of new roads and 4,800 km (3,000 miles) of highways had been built.

1939 Hitler invaded Poland. World War II began.

1940 Sir Winston Leonard Spencer Churchill (1875-1965) became Conservative Prime Minister and war leader in England. He served until 1945, when he was defeated in the general election. He served again as Prime Minister from 1951 to 1955. He wrote several books of history, and was awarded the Nobel prize for literature in 1953.

1941 Hitler launched Operation Barbarossa.

1941 Under pressure from the British and Soviets, and because of his pro-Nazi sentiments, Reza Shah Pahlavi was forced to abdicate in favor of his twenty–one–year–old son, Mohammad Reza.
Reza Shah's success was limited, and curtailed by the Second World War. Like many nationalists, he was more intent on the independence of his country than on the freedom of its people, wanting his compatriots to be proud of their fatherland rather than of their liberties. But as a result of his single-minded determination, Iran was able to achieve considerable progress.

1942 The Iranian Communist Party, outlawed by Reza Shah, once again appeared under the name of 'Tudeh Party'.
The abdication of Reza Shah removed the principal source of stability. Tribes asserted themselves, clerics strove to regain lost ground, and political parties emerged in profusion.

1942 Iran, Britain and the Soviet Union signed the Tripartite Treaty allowing them to stay in Iran during the course of the war.

By the terms of the treaty, Iran conceded to the Allies the right for the transit of war material through the country provided that their presence did not constitute an 'occupation'. The USA, invited to join later that year, declined.

____ According to the Tripartite Treaty, Iran declared war on Germany and Japan, and subsequently entered the United Nations.

1943 Fedaiyan Islam, a small politico-religious group, was founded and remained active until 1955. It tried to enforce Muslim laws and attacked politicians with foreign connections.

1943 Dr Mohammad Mosaddeq was elected into the assembly.
During the Allied occupation, Mosaddeq formulated the 'negative equilibrium' principle, calling for Iran to establish its independence.

1945 Two Soviet-instrument Communist parties had formed in Iran: Tudeh and Ferqeh Demokrat.
Tudeh leadership represented the usual picture of Western oriented Marxist ideology. Ferqeh Demokrat reflected the circumstances special to Azerbaijan province. They functioned as separate parties.

1945 Second World War ended in September.

1946 Seyyed Ahmad Kasravi Tabrizi (b.1890), Iranian historian, linguist, jurist and ideologist, died.
Charges of slander of Islam were brought against him because of his views on religion. He was assassinated by the Fedaiyan Islam.

1947 Mosaddeq was re-elected into the assembly.

1948 Mohandas Karamchand Gandhi (b.1869), Indian statesman, died. He led the Indian struggle to win independence from British rule. His philosophy of non-violence influenced people all over the world and won him the title 'Mahatma' ("Great Soul"). He was assassinated shortly after Indian independence.

1950 Dr Mosaddeq established the National Front, a loose association of diverse political groups.

1951 Sadeq Hedayat (b.1903), innovative writer of modern Iran, died.

His daring experiments in technique and in thought have exercised a powerful influence on the development of modern Iranian fiction.

1951 Prime Minister Ali Razmara was assassinated.

The Assembly passed legislation for the nationalization of the Anglo-Iranian Oil Company.

1951 Prime Minister Mohammad Mosaddeq came to power

During a course of two years, Mosaddeq nationalized Iranian oil, moved to limit Shah's power, and reduced the role of foreign interests.

1953 The nationalist movement forced the Shah to leave the country for Rome. American and British Intelligence orchestrated riots, brought down the Mosaddeq government, and allowed the Shah to return to Tehran.

1953 Soviet leader Joseph Stalin (b.1879) died. He was the successor of Lenin and went on to become the virtual dictator of the USSR.

1955 Albert Einstein (b.1879, possibly the greatest scientist of the twentieth century, died.

1957 Aqa Khan III died and was followed by his son Aqa Khan IV.

1957 Martial law was abolished and the Savak or 'State Intelligence and Security Organization' assumed responsibility for internal security.

1960 Communist parties of Tudeh and Ferqeh Demokrat united.

1960 Nima Yushij (b.1897), Iranian poet, died.

His most important work is a long poem, entitled 'Myth', containing a dialogue between a dismayed lover and the Myth, which consoles him. The poem may be said to have heralded the beginning of modernism in Persian poetry.

1960 Ruhollah Khomeini (R) received the title of Grand Ayatollah, thereby making him one of the supreme religious leaders of the Shia community in Iran.
As a Shia scholar, Ayatollah Khomeini (R) produced numerous writings on Islamic philosophy, law, and ethics, but it was his outspoken opposition to the Shah, his denunciations of Western influences, and his uncompromising advocacy of Islamic purity that won him his initial following in Iran.

1961 Haji Aqa Hossein Tabatabai Borujerdi (b.1875), the greatest religious authority of the Shia world in his time, died.
Under his guidance, the Qom Circle for Religious Studies became the most important clerical center of Shi'ism. He was also concerned with Sunni-Shia relations and entered into correspondence with al-Azhar rectors in Egypt.

1961 Mohammad Reza Shah launched the White Revolution to further modernize Iran's economy and social infrastructure, including land reform and women's rights.

1962 Ayatollah Abol Qasim Kashani, a politically active Iranian mojtahed and a supporter of Mosaddeq, died.

1963 Ayatollah Khomeini (R) launched a campaign to oppose The Shah's reforms. After calling for Iranians to rise against the monarchy, he was imprisoned. His ensuing arrest sparked antigovernment riots.

1964 Ayatollah Khomeini (R) was forcibly exiled from Iran on Nov. 4.
He eventually settled in the Shia holy city of Najaf, Southern Iraq, from where he continued to call for the Shah's overthrow and the establishment of an Islamic Republic in Iran.

1967 Mosaddeq (b.1882), Iranian nationalist politician and Prime Minister, died.

1968 Martin Luther King (b.1929), black American clergyman and civil rights leader, was assassinated in Memphis. His powerful and moving speeches inspired the movement for black equality.

1969 Seyyed Jalal Al-e Ahmad (b.1923), Iranian prose writer and ideologist, died.

He wrote literary fiction, essays and reports, and regional monographs.

1970 The Second Academy, or Farhangestan, was formed.

1973 Pablo Picasso (b.1881), Spanish painter and pioneer of cubism, died.

1975 Iran and Iraq signed The Algiers Agreement whereby the line of deepest water in the Arvand River (the Shatt al-Arab) was taken to be the international boundary between the two countries.

1978 Uprising against the Shah spread throughout the country.

1978 Under pressure from Tehran, Iraq's ruler Saddam Hussein, forced Ayatollah Khomeini (R) to leave Iraq on Oct. 6. He then settled in Neauphle-le-Château, a suburb of Paris.

From there his supporters relayed his tape-recorded messages to an increasingly aroused Iranian populace.

1979 Massive demonstrations, strikes, and civil unrest forced the departure of the Shah from the country on January 16.

1979 Ayatollah Khomeini (R) returned from exile to a triumphant welcome.

1979 Iranians overwhelmingly voted for the establishment of an Islamic Republic.

This marked the end of centuries of monarchy in Iran.

A year later the Shah passed away in exile.

Glossary

(A) Pronounced 'Alaih-e Salam', Peace Be Upon Him, or 'Alaih-a Salam', Peace Be Upon Her. An expression of high respect used for the twelve Imams of the Shias and their family and the Old and the New Testament Prophets.

Abbasids Caliphs of Baghdad, 750-1258.

Achaemenians Royal dynasty whose name derives from the first of the line, Achaemenes, 700 BC.

Ahriman Power of evil and darkness, twin to Ahura Mazda, the good spirit, with whom he is constantly at war.

Ahura Mazda 'The Wise Lord', The Great God, the incarnation of goodness, and supreme deity of Zoroastrians.

Anahita 'The Immaculate', goddess of the waters and fertility and associated with warfare.

Anatolia Turkish Anadolu, also called Asia Minor, the peninsula of land that today constitutes the Asiatic portion of Turkey.

Apadana Large audience hall in Achaemenian palaces.

Arsacids A name often given to members of the Parthian dynasty, founded by Arsaces.

Assyria Kingdom of northern Mesopotamia that became the center of one of the great empires of the ancient Middle East. It was located in what is now northern Iraq and southeastern Turkey.

Avesta Collection of the sacred books of Zoroastrianism.

Ayatollah An honorific title for theologians as a fully qualified Muslim Jurist of superior learning.

Babylon One of the most famous cities of antiquity. It was the capital of southern Mesopotamia (Babylonia) from the early 2nd millennium to the early 1st millennium BC and capital of the Neo-Babylonian Empire in the 7th and 6th centuries BC, when it was at the height of its splendor.

Babylonia Ancient cultural region occupying southeastern Mesopotamia between the Tigris and Euphrates rivers (modern southern Iraq from around Baghdad to the Persian Gulf).

Bactria Bactriana, or Zariaspa, ancient country lying between the mountains of the Hindu Kush and the Amu Darya (ancient Oxus River) in what is now part of Afghanistan, Uzbekistan, and Tajikistan.

Barrel Vault Semicircular vault.

Barsom Bundle of twigs tied together symbolizing vegetal life in Zoroastrian ceremonies.

Buyids Islamic dynasty of Persian descent, also known as Dailamites, 932-1056.

Byzantine Empire The eastern half of the Roman Empire, which survived for a thousand years after the western half had crumbled into various feudal kingdoms and which finally fell to Ottoman Turkish onslaughts in 1453.

Byzantium Later Constantinople, modern Istanbul, ancient Greek city on the shore of the Bosporus; also, an alternative name for the Byzantine Empire, which had its capital at Constantinople.

Caliph 'Successor', a title initially referring to the first four successors to the Prophet (S), who assumed his administrative and political but not religious functions, and later used to refer to the rulers of the Muslim Empire.

Capadocia Ancient district in east-central Anatolia in the rugged plateau north of the Taurus Mountains, Turkey, important as a Roman ally, client, and later province.

Chahar Taq 'Four Arches', open-sided pavilion with four pillars supporting a domed roof, displaying the Zoroastrian sacred fire to the public in the Sassanian period,
224-651.

Ctesiphon Tusbun, or Taysafun, ancient city located on the left (northeast) bank of the Tigris River about 20 miles (32 km) southeast of modern Baghdad, in east-central Iraq.

Cuneiform Wedge-shaped writing used in ancient Persia.

Dakhme 'Tower of Silence', usually a high enclosure on a hilltop, inside which were exposed the corpse of the Zoroastrians.

Delos An ancient center of religious, political, and commercial life in the Aegean Sea in Greece.

Ecbatana Ancient city on the site of which stands the modern city of Hamadan, Iran. Ecbatana was the capital of Media and was subsequently the summer residence of the Achaemenian kings and one of the residences of the Parthian kings.

Edessa An ancient city in Macedonia, Greece.

Elamites A people who dominated the Iranian plateau, 4500-640 BC.

Elymais Ancient Parthian vassal state located east of the lower Tigris River and usually considered part of the larger district of Susiana. It incorporated much of the area of the biblical region of Elam, approximately equivalent to the modern region of Khuzestan, Iran.

Ephesus The most important Greek city in Ionian Asia Minor, the ruins of which lie in western Turkey.

Griffin A composite monster with the features of an eagle and a lion.

Hadith The spoken traditions attributed to the Prophet Mohammad (S), which are revered and received in Islam as a major source of religious law and moral guidance.

Hatra modern Al-Hadr, ancient city between the Tigris and Euphrates rivers in present-day northern Iraq.

Hecatempolis The Parthians second capital, 32 km (20 miles) west of Damghan.

Hegira Prophet Mohammad (S)'s migration of 622 from Mecca to Medina; the date represents the starting point of the Muslim era.

Hellespont Now Dardanelles is a narrow strait in north-western Turkey, 61 km (38 miles) long, linking the Aegean Sea with the Sea of Marmara.

Hypostyle In architecture, interior space whose roof rests on pillars or columns.

Hyrcania Old Persian Varkana ("Wolf's Land"), ancient region located southeast of the Caspian Sea. Its capital was Zadracarta (Astrabad, modern Gorgan in Iran), and it formed part of the Median, Achaemenian, Seleucid, and Parthian empires, either as an independent province or joined with Parthia.

Il-Khan	A Mongol title referring to a Mongol ruler reigning on part of the empire as a vassal of the Emperor.
Imam	'Spiritual leader', prayer leader; Ali (A) and 11 of his descendants; leader of the Shia community.
Istakhr	Ancient city near Persepolis, which became the center of the Sassanian Empire in the 3rd century.
Ivan	Barrel-vaulted hall whose fourth side is open onto a courtyard.
Jame Mosque	A Friday Mosque. Often the largest or the best equipped mosque in any given town or city to hold the Friday Prayer led by Imam Jum'e, prayer leader.
Karbala	A city in central Iraq where the Battle of Karbala was fought in 680.
Khanegah	Dervish monastery or retreat house.
Khorasan	Historical region and realm comprising a vast territory now lying in northeastern Iran, southern Turkmenistan, and northern Afghanistan.
Kufa	A city in Iraq founded in 638 by Umar, the second Caliph, as a garrison town.

Kufic	Angular form of Islamic calligraphy extensively used in the first five centuries of Islam.
Kushans	A people of Iranian origin who ruled over a vast empire including Afghanistan, northern India, southern Russia, and Chinese Turkestan, 1st-3rd century AD.
Madrasseh	Theological college usually attached to a mosque.
Manichaeism	Dualistic religious movement founded in Persia in the 3rd century AD by Mani or Manes.
Massagetaes	Ancient confederation of nomadic hordes east of the Caspian.
Mazdakism	Dualistic religion that rose to prominence in the late 5th century in Iran from obscure origins. According to some scholars, Mazdakism was a reform movement seeking an optimistic interpretation of the Manichaean dualism.
Mecca	Mecca is the most holy city of Islam in western Saudi Arabia; it was the birthplace of the Prophet Mohammad (S), and is a religious center to which Muslims attempt a pilgrimage, or hajj, at least once during their lifetime.
Media	Ancient kingdom of western Iran whose capital was Ecbatana, now in Hamadan, 700-550 BC.

Medina One of the two most sacred cities of Islam, situated in the Hejaz region of western Saudi Arabia about 160 km (100 miles) inland from the Red Sea and some 447 km (278 miles) from Mecca by road.

Merv Ancient city of Central Asia lying near the modern town of Mary, Turkmenistan.

Mesopotamia Mesopotamia, a Greek term meaning "Land Between the Rivers", is the region between the Tigris and Euphrates in Iraq.

Mihrab The niche in the Qibla wall of a mosque, facing Mecca, and to which the faithful face when praying. Often elaborately decorated for emphasis.

Minaret 'Tower', from which the call to prayer is made, and either attached to, or close by, a mosque.

Minbar Pulpit of wood or stone.

Mithras Ancient Persian god of light and the sun, of contracts, justice, prosperity and victory, and one of the three judges of the souls of the dead.

Mobed Magus, a Zoroastrian priest.

Muharram Muslim lunar month regarded as a period of mourning by the Shia sect, in commemoration of the martyrdom of Imam Hussein (A) at the battle of Karbala.

Mujtahid A theologian having the authority to issue Fatwah, or religious decree.

Muqarnas Architectural detail decorating domes, vaults and ivans composed into a 'honeycomb' design.

Naskh A cursive form of calligraphy, which gradually replaced Kufic from the eleventh century onwards.

Nisa Parthaunisa, first capital of the Parthians, 18 km (12 miles), northwest of modern Ashgabat or Ashkhabad, the capital of Turkmenistan.

Nisibis An ancient city, which is now Urfa and Nusaybin in southeast Turkey.

Olama Plural of Alem, all knowing, scholars trained in Islamic theology and law.

Pahlavi Language of pre-Islamic Persia under the Parthians and Sassanids.

Parthia A province of Iran southeast of the Caspian Sea. The name was applied to the whole of Persia during the reign of the Parthian dynasty, 270 BC-224 AD.

Peloponnesus Peloponnese, small peninsula of 21,000 square km (8,000 square miles), jutting southward into the Mediterranean that since antiquity has been a major region of Greece.

Phoenicia	Ancient region corresponding to modern Lebanon, with adjoining parts of modern Syria and Palestine. Its inhabitants, the Phoenicians, were notable merchants, traders, and colonizers of the Mediterranean in the 1st millennium BC. The chief cities of Phoenicia (excluding colonies) were Sidon, Tyre, and Berot (modern Beirut).
Pliny the younger	Roman author and administrator (61-113 AD) who left a collection of private letters of great literary charm, intimately illustrating public and private life in the heyday of the Roman Empire.
Pol	Bridge.
Qibla	Direction of the sacred shrine of the Kaaba in Mecca, toward which Muslims turn five times each day when performing the Salat (daily ritual prayer).
Qur'an	The sacred scripture of Islam, regarded by Muslims as the Infallible Word of God, revealed to Prophet Mohammad (S) over a period of 20 years.
Quraysh	Ruling tribe of Mecca at the time of the birth of the Prophet Mohammad (S) consisting of ten main clans.
(R)	Pronounced 'Rahmat ol-Lah Alaih', Blessing Be Upon Him, and 'Rahmat ol-Lah Alaiha' Blessing Be Upon Her. An expression of high consideration for deceased religious figures.

(S) Pronounced 'Sal al-Lah Alaih-e va All-ehi va Sal-lam, Praise Be Upon Him and his Progeny. An expression of highest reverence exclusively used for the Prophet Mohammad (S).

Satrap Provincial governor in the Achaemenian Empire.

Scythians Members of a nomadic people originally of Iranian stock who migrated from Central Asia to southern Russia in the 8th and 7th centuries BC. Centered on what is now the Crimea, the Scythians founded a rich, powerful empire that survived for several centuries before succumbing to the Sarmatians during the 4th century BC to the 2nd century AD.

Seistan Sistan, extensive border region, eastern Iran and southwestern Afghanistan.

Seleucia on the Tigris Greek Seleukeia, Hellenistic city founded by Seleucus I Nicator (r.312-281 BC) as his eastern capital; it replaced Babylon as Mesopotamia's leading city and was closely associated with the spread of Hellenistic culture in Mesopotamia.

Sheikh 'Wise man', an Islamic title given to men of religious prominence.

Shi'ism A sect of Islam formed immediately after the demise of the prophet over the question of succession.

Shia Member of the smaller of the two major branches of Islam, distinguished from the majority Sunnis, supporting the succession of Ali (A) after the Prophet Mohammad (S).

Squinch A section of vaulted masonry bridging an angle of a rectangular room often used to create a circular base for the dome.

Stucco Carved or molded plaster often painted and used as an ornamental and protective covering of walls, widely used by Parthians and Sassanians.

Sufi A Muslim seeking the spiritual path, or 'Tariqat', the esoteric dimension of Islam, to achieve mystic union with God.

Sufism Mystic Islamic belief and practice in which followers seek to find divine love and knowledge through direct personal experience of God.

Sultan A title used by Muslim sovereigns since the 11th century.

Sunnism The orthodox branch of Islam believing in the four elected Caliphs as successors to the prophet (S).

Transoxiana Transoxania, is a historical region of Turkestan in Central Asia east of the Amu Darya (Oxus River) and west of the Syr Darya (Jaxartes River), roughly corresponding to present-day Uzbekistan and parts of Turkmenistan and Kazakhstan.

Triumvirate A ruling group of three people in ancient Rome.

True Cross Reputedly the wood of the cross on which Jesus Christ (A) was crucified.

Urartu Powerful kingdom that flourished around Lake Van in Turkey and Lake Uromiyeh in northwestern Iran.

Vizier Minister.

Ziggurat Mesopotamian name for a staged temple composed of multiple tiers and resembling an artificial mountain. The Biblical Tower of Babel was a Ziggurat.

Zoroaster Zarathustra, prophet and founder of the Zoroastrian religion.

Zoroastrianism Ancient pre-Islamic religion of Iran based on message of Prophet Zoroaster that survives in isolated areas and more prosperously in India, where the descendents of Zoroastrian Iranian (Persian) immigrants are known as Parsis, or Parsees. Containing both monotheistic and dualistic features, this religion influenced other major religions. Implications of Zoroastrianism means a code of ethics based on good thoughts, good words and good deeds.

Appendix 1
Major Archaeological Sites

Teppeh **Ali Kosh**
The inhabitants of Teppeh Ali Kosh built their large houses around 6200-5800 BC. These were built of handmade bricks. The rooms were quite spacious - 10x16 feet. In some instances there were indications that the floors had also been clay surfaced. All the bricks had been made from local mud, cut into approximate rectangles, and sun dried.

Anshan
The site first flourished as the capital of South Elam.
40 km (25 miles) north of Shiraz and west of Persepolis at a place called Talle Maaliyan lie the ruins of the ancient city of Anshan with defensive walls encircling an area of more than 1,000 hectares. Anshan was later inhabited by the Persians, and was the place of coronation of Cyrus the Great as the king of one branch of the Persians in 559 BC.

Talle **Bakun**
Talle Bakun black on buff pottery, some of which were in form of conical vessels, appeared around mid-fifth millennium BC. At the two mounds of Talle Bakun, 2.5 km (1.7 miles) south of Persepolis, there is also evidence of textile production.

Bishapur
Following his successive victories over three Roman emperors, Gordian, Philip the Arab, and Valerian, Shapur had the vast city constructed by some 70,000 Roman captives of the victory over Valerian. The city complex of Palaces, Anahita Fire Temple, and houses could have had as many as 80,000 inhabitants. The most impressive part of the excavated portion is the 20 square meter central palace sided by 4 triple-vaulted ivans, which may have

supported a giant dome. The floors of the two neighboring palaces to the east and west of the main palace were covered by stone in the middle and mosaic for the margin.

Cheshmeh Ali

Situated in Reyy, south Tehran, Cheshmeh Ali has produced some of the earliest and finest painted pottery of the area. Reddish-orange pottery unearthed here from very early 4th millennium BC have sophisticated black and brown patterns, and sometimes were coated with a slip.
Later Parthian and Sassanian occupations have been proven here as well as a 19th century bas-relief left by Fath Ali Shah of Qajar dynasty.

Teppeh **Chogha Mish**

Situated 27 km (17 miles) east of Susa, Chogha Mish flourished in the 6th and 5th millennia BC, dominating the 3,200 square km plain of Susa. The importance of the site lies in the fact that it is probably the only settlement of the plain having uninterrupted habitation from ca.7000 BC, and an early industrial center. A larger city dominated the whole mound from 5th mill. BC covering an area of 20 hectares (50 acres). Pottery including storage jars, tiny perfume holders, vases with reliefs, brilliantly patterned burnished pottery, cylinder seal impressions on clay, one depicting musicians and a singer, are among the discovered artifacts. Evidence of a fire destroying a mansion of middle Susiana period has also come to light. Chogha Mish was also occupied during Achaemenian and Parthian Periods.

Chogha Zanbil

The world's best preserved and architecturally unique ziggurat of Chogha Zanbil, situated 40 km (25 miles) southeast of Susa, was constructed together with the city of Dur-Untashi in 1250 BC by

Untash Hoban as a religious complex jointly dedicated to Inshushinak, ("Lord of Susa"), and Naparisha ("Lord of Anshan"). The ziggurat measuring 100x100 m (330x330 ft) at the base served as both temple and tomb, composed of five separately built concentric levels of varying elevation, each independently constructed directly from the ground. A temple capped the top where the most important cultic rituals were performed. The monument was constructed using fired bricks for the casing of the structure and sun-dried bricks as filler. The exterior of the monument was decorated with glittering blue and green glazed fire bricks, inlaid ivory mosaics, as well as opaque glass mosaics depicting prancing creatures. On both sides of the entrance gate to the enclosure were placed guardian bulls, probably the personification of Inshushinak, and winged griffins glazed in terracotta. Around the main ziggurat were other cultic shrines of which the T-shaped temple of Nabu is architecturally dissimilar. The close-by tomb chambers here bear resemblance to those of Haft Teppeh, with one of city walls a short distance behind.

Talle **Eblis**

The site, southeast of Bardsir and near the village of Fakhrabad, was settled by people who continued to occupy it until around 1000 BC. The most significant fact is the smelting and casting of copper from ore, carried out as early as late fifth millennium BC and possibly earlier. The inhabitants here were in trade and cultural connection with Sialk to the north, Talle Bakun to the southwest, and Mesopotamia to the west.

Firuzabad

Originally called Ardashir Khoreh ("Glory of Ardashir"), or Gur, the city was constructed by Ardashir, the founder of the Sassanian Empire, following his victory over Parthian king Artabanus V. In the center of the site there stands a square tower, whose function has not yet been satisfactorily explained. A short distance to the northeast of the tower is a building with two intact domes, usually referred to as Ardashir's Fire Temple, which is the earliest example of Sassanian architecture and the Iranian dome.

Ganj Teppeh

Situated 10 km (6 miles) west of Harsin and 1 km (0.6 miles) north of the village of Khurvin, Ganj Teppeh is one of the earliest sites of permanent settlement in Western Iran. The oldest pottery of Neolithic Period in Iran, dated 8450 BC by carbon 14 test, was recovered here. It is dark gray and fired at a low temperature.

Teppeh **Ghabrestan**

Situated 8 km (5 miles)north of Sagzabad village in the plain of Qazvin, the site was occupied from mid-sixth millennium BC. The discovery of a large house with nine rooms around a central yard has suggested the existence of a governing body at this time. Two copper smelting furnaces and casts as well as pottery workshops have also been identified. Concurrent with Sialk IV and V, houses with two to four rooms were common at Teppeh Ghabrestan.

Gudin Teppeh

Situated 13 km (9 miles) east of Kangaver, Gudin Teppeh, the once extensively occupied site of the Bronze Age, was re-occupied after a long interval of five centuries. Two columned halls from this period of Median occupation make the link between the columned halls at Hasanlu, the oldest columned halls identified in Iran from late 13 century BC, and those at the palaces of Cyrus the Great at Pasargadae.

Haft Teppeh

Haft Teppeh, with its visible 14 main mounds, rests 10 km (6 miles) southeast of Susa. Constructed by Elamite king Tepti Ahar as a royal complex of ziggurats, palaces, temples and royal tombs in mid 14th century BC, it adorned the flourishing city of Tikni. The two royal tombs probably hold the world's first vaulted roofs, predating the arches of Chogha Zanbil by about 2 centuries. Within the two royal tombs 35 skeletons as well as a clay sarcophagus covered with bitumen and containing burial urns was unearthed. In the construction of the complex baked and sun-dried clay bricks were used, clay and gypsum mortar being applied between them respectively. Gypsum was also used to plaster the walls which helped to keep the bricks dry from the high subterranean water level. Earlier remains that have been uncovered include coarse pottery from 6th mill. BC, and painted pottery from 5th, mid 4th and 2nd millennia BC. A wall from early third millennium BC. was also among the finds.

Hassanlu

The 25 m (80 ft) high mound lies 85 km (52 miles) south of Urumiya and 7 km (5 miles) north of Naqadeh. Ten periods of occupation have been attested here, the oldest being dated around 6th mill. BC and the latest contemporary to late Sassanian period. In the 13th century BC, a citadel was built on the already existing levels. The buildings of this period were made in stone, with the three columned halls being the earliest such halls yet identified on the plateau. The citadel's defensive walls, 7 m (23 ft) high and 3 m (10 ft) thick, had bastions spaced at 30 m (100 ft) intervals. There were streets, public buildings, grand stairways, porticos and two or three storey high mud-brick houses, rendering Hassanlu the most significant early Iron age site of Western Iran. The most notable item unearthed here was what has become known as the Hassanlu cup, measuring 21 cm (8.5 inches) in height, 25 cm (12 inches) in diameter and 900 grams in weight in gold, dating from 1200 BC. The citadel met its end around 500 BC.

Hecmatana

The mound, now part of the modern city of Hamadan, was the site of the capital of the Medes set up by Diocus, the founder of the Median Empire, on the site of the previously Kassite city of Kar-Kassi around the end of the 8th century BC. It was described by Greeks as a fortified city with seven concentric walls, the innermost two covered in gold and silver. It later became the summer capital of the Persian Empire. Many seasons of excavation have revealed a network of houses and streets and artifacts from early times down to the Islamic Period.

Ismail Abad Teppeh

Ismail Abad or Musellan (Mushelan) Teppeh is situated 36 km (22 miles) southwest of Tehran in the plain of Shahriyar. Two levels were uncovered here. Pottery from 4th mill. BC in both levels was red with black geometric patterns, with human and animal shapes found in the top level, both types bearing resemblance to Cheshmeh Ali pottery. The dead were laid in the grave lying squatted on either the left or right side of the body facing the east with their hands on their chests, which may indicate a form of Mithraistic belief amongst the dwellers. The dead were left food in the grave, but no trace of any weapon of any kind has been found, with only evidence of farming or animal husbandry unearthed.

Kangavar

About 90 km (55 miles) west of Hamadan on the road to Kermanshah sits the site of Kangavar, believed to have been an Anahita temple. Like Persepolis, a platform had first been constructed in Achaemenian times to accommodate the Anahita temple, where Artaxexes II is believed to have been crowned in 404 BC. Evidence from recent excavations indicate the temple's construction techniques as Iranian rather than Greek, as it had originally been thought, based on the fact that a Greek settlement had been established close by in Seleucid times.

Persepolis

55 km (36 miles) north of Shiraz by road rests the Achaemenian ceremonial site of Parsa or Persepolis. Made on the side of Mount Rahmat or Mithras on an artificial platform, the first palace of the

complex, the Apadana, was begun by Darius in 518 BC to be followed by palaces and gates built by later Achaemenian kings. The most notable of the monuments are Gate of all Nations, the throne hall of Xerxes, and the private palaces of Darius I, Xerxes, and Artaxerxes II. In the construction of the site, the very best materials and workmanship of the empire were employed: cedar wood from Lebanon, Lapis Lazuli from Afghanistan, ivory from Ethiopia, etc, to achieve an eclectic innovation in architecture that remained unrivalled. On 21st of March of each year, satraps from all over the empire came to celebrate the onset of spring and offer tribute to the King of Kings. The Eastern Staircase of the Apadana Palace has in carving the scene of 23 representative delegations bearing tribute to the king on the occasion of vernal equinox, when Persians celebrate the new year. The site was destroyed by fire around 330 BC, marking the end of the 220 glorious years of the first Persian Empire.

Qasr-e Shirin

The Sassanian palace of Qasr-e Shirin lies 20 km (14 miles) northeast of the border town of Khosravi. According to local belief, the palace was constructed by Khosrow II (r.590-628) for his Christian Queen Shirin. The palace had a typical Sassanian plan similar to the palace of Ardashir in Firuzabad, with an Achaemenian style staircase forming the approach to the terrace on which the main palace and supporting buildings were constructed. East Roman Emperor Heraclius is held responsible for the destruction of the palace following his short-lived victories in the area in 628 AD.

Shahr-e Sukhteh

The 150-hectare site, formed around 3200 BC near Zabul, has so far produced tens of thousands of stone tools; over two million potsherds; and thousands of unfired clay figurines, broken at the time of making probably as a religious gesture; gray pottery with red patterns and gray pottery with black patterns; great quantity of Jewelry made from Lapis Lazuli, turquoise and carnelian; a tablet in proto-Elamite; the remains of a large mansion covering an area of 650 square meters, destroyed around 1800 BC; female's flat and cylinder seals that reveal women's active role in social and political spheres, and 25,000 or more graves.

Teppeh **Sialk**

It comprises two mounds: northern mound, described as one of the earliest settlements on the Iranian plateau, housing Sialks I and II settlements from 5800-5500 to 4300 BC, and southern mound, formed 800 meters away to the south after a fire had destroyed the northern village, housing Sialks III, IV and V settlements from 4300 onwards. At Sialk, the dead were painted in red ochre and buried in the floor of their homes. Among the remains is a seal with a proto-Elamite inscription in the layers of Sialk IV, and the earliest depiction of a Near-Eastern man. The latter is in the form of a knife handle shaped like a man wearing a wrap around the waist and a cap. The use of a rough potters' wheel and earliest forged copper tools have been ascertained. The settlement evidently consisted of huts made of tree branches, though the inhabitants were practicing rudimentary garden culture and had domesticated oxen and sheep.

Susa

Lying north of Ahvaz, Susa was inhabited from 4200 BC. The mound lies on the left bank of Shaur river, stretching 1500 m (5000 ft) north to south.

On the mound rest the Acropolis, Royal Town, Palace of Darius, the Apadana, and the fortress of the French Archeological Mission, as well as other buildings including, temple tombs.

On the Acropolis, an estimated 2,000 human remains from late 5th to 4th mill. BC have been recovered buried with funerary items. The pottery here is dark-painted buff ware and red and buff plain wares. Seals in great quantity were also found having both geometric and figural scenes. Susa's decline came around 700 BC, probably as a result of exhausting wars with Assyria, before the final blow that was dealt to it by the Assyrian king Ashurbanipal shortly before 640 BC.

Teppeh **Yahya**

The mound resting 225 km (160 miles) south of Kerman in Soughan valley dates to late Neolithic Period in the deepest layer. The homes at this stage were small and of sun-dried brick. Unfinished seals identical to those known as Persian Gulf seals and unfinished steatite bowls with incised hut-shaped motifs which had previously been associated with Mesopotamia and Susa were found at the site. These unfinished bowls and a quarried steatite mine nearby have convinced some that the items mentioned had been exported from here. There were also 30 blank writing tablets and seven inscribed in proto-Elamite giving rise to the idea that the written tablets were the work of locals at Teppeh Yahya itself. Teppeh Yahya's trade connections with the Indus valley, the Persian Gulf, and Mesopotamia in the third millennium BC has been determined. The area flourished from mid-third millennium BC.

Yannik Teppeh

The mound, 20 km (14 miles) southwest of Tabriz, revealed red pottery with simple patterns dating from mid-fourth millennium BC. Grey pottery, presumably brought in by settlers from Anatolia and the Caucasus to Yannik Teppeh, has been found as far east as Teppeh Hessar near Damghan.

Teppeh **Zagheh**

Located 60 km (37 miles) south of Qazvin and 23 km (14 miles) northwest of Sagzabad, Zagheh is the oldest settlement of the Qazvin plain, inhabited at least from the last quarter of the 7th mill. BC. down to late 6th mill. BC, when it was abandoned. The dating has been based on C14 tests carried out on items found about a third of the way down to the virgin soil. Amongst the numerous retrieved items were 7th and 6th mill. BC pottery, storage vessels, figurines, tools and knobbed pottery from 6th and 5th mill. BC. Two-roomed houses with hearths as well as metal smelting kilns were identified in the layer corresponding to 5th mill. BC. The floors of houses and workshops were finely plastered over. Intramural burials were commonplace with the corpses painted in red ochre.

Teppeh **Ziviyeh**

40 km (25 miles) east of Saqqez lies the first millennium site of Ziviyeh, destroyed by Sargon II around 714 BC. In his inscription, Sargon II mentions two other cities which he had burned: Izirtu and Aramaied, Izirtu being the Mannaean capital. A sarcophagus found at Ziviyeh carries depictions of men wearing pointed hats and bearing tribute. Inside, items such as gold chest plaques, engraved ivory plaques, gold and silver swords and fibulae were found, all probably dating from the last quarter of the 7th century BC. Excavations carried out from 1976 by Iranian archaeologists revealed a huge building with numerous objects mostly belonging to 6th century BC. Apart from pottery, rhytons of different kinds, glazed vessels (boot-shaped pottery), gold ibex and eagle head figurines, gold jewelry and a number of other miscellaneous objects were also recovered.

Appendix 2
Major Prehistoric Events

4500 The Elamites, the first people of the plateau to have a distinct culture, language and religion, began to flourish.

The Elamites were a great nation neither of Indo-European origin, like the Iranians, nor Semitic.

____ Sumerians, a non-Semitic people probably of the Iranian plateau, settled southern parts of Mesopotamia, forming a nation of city-states.

By early 4th millennium BC they had formed the greatest cities of the world, with Ur and Sumer being the most notable. Their civilization gave rise to the Akkadian dynasty formed by Sargon I in ca.2340 BC. The decline of the Sumerians came at the turn of 2nd millennium BC. They were subsequently assimilated by Mesopotamian powers that were rising in the area.

3000 The first pictographic script was invented by the Sumerians.

2900 The first Elamite kingdom was formed by Avan dynasty.

They greatly developed urban civilization under orderly government, and developed their own art of hand writing, a pictographic script known as proto-Elamite, in early third millennium BC. Their empire was to wax and wane in their southwestern heartland over many centuries.

2300 The first Elamite linear script was invented.

2300 In a peace treaty written in Elamite cuneiform between Naram Sin, king of Akkad, and Khita, king of Elam, mutual power and respect was recognized.

____ Kassites occupied areas to the southwest of the Caspian and gradually advanced south to the present day Lurestan Province.

Ecbatana, the later Median capital was constructed on top of the Kassite city of Kar-kassi. Although the Kassites' racial background is not clear, some of the names of their deities are similar to those of Indo-Aryans'. Lurestan Bronzes found mainly around Harsin have been attributed to the Kassites.

____ Lullubis occupied an area extending from lake Urumiyeh to Saqqiz, where they reached the height of their civilization.
Lullubis constantly contended with the Assyrians and were finally destroyed by them in the second millennium BC.

2100 Lullubi king Annubanini made what is probably the oldest existing rock carving in Western Iran at Sar-e Pol-e Zahab.

____ Goths ruled what is now Azerbaijan and Kurdestan in the third and second millennia BC.
A rock carving similar to that of Annubanini's remains from the same period

2005 Ebcin, the last king of the third dynasty of Ur, was carried as captive to Elam following his defeat by the Elamites.

1750 The Kassites occupied Babylon and began their 577 years of domination.
Some scholars have proposed that the Kassites may have been high-land Elamites.

1730 King of Elam, Kutir Nahunte imposed a severe defeat on the Akkadians.

____ Mittanis conquered an area stretching from the Mediterranean to Azerbaijan and the Zagros Range.
Their first capital of Vashuganni was moved to Arrapkha near Kirkuk in present day Iraq. They assimilated the Hurrians and Goths and were instrumental in the unification of Egypt, resulting in many Pharaohs marrying Mittani princesses.

____ Mannaeans united to form a kingdom from present day Maragheh to parts of Iranian Kurdestan.
They were at constant loggerheads with Assyrians who after their military successes drafted Mannaean artisans, especially those excelling in pottery, metallurgy and architecture, to work in Assyria.
Mannaeans were mainly farmers and cattle-breaders partly owing to the fertile areas they occupied. The major mounds of Ziwiyeh, Hassanlu and Qelaychi may have been sites of their settlements. Their demise came with the rise of the Medes in the first decade of 7 century BC.

____ Vedas were composed.

Vedas were sacred hymns or verses composed in archaic Sanskrit and current among the Indo-European-speaking peoples who entered India from the Iranian regions.

1374 Tepti Ahar, the Elamite king, defeated Kadashman Enlil, king of the Kassites, liberating territory previously lost to the Assyrians.

1250 Elamite king Untash Huban or Untash Gal (r.1265-1245 BC), of Ighalki dynasty, founded the city of Dur-Untashi with the ziggurat of Chogha-Zanbil at its heart, jointly dedicated to the Lord of Susa, Inshushinak, and Naparisha, Lord of Anshan.

1160 Shutruk Nahunte, king of Elam (r.1180-1155 BC), defeated Babylonians on several occasions taking many items, including steles of Hamurabi of Assyria and Naram Sin of Akkad to the Elamite capital of Susa.

1155 Kutir Nahunte II crushed a revolt by Babylonians who had been subjugated by his father Shutruk Nahunte.

____ The Indo-European Medes and Persians entered the plateau by routes around the Caspian Sea.

____ The Medes were the first Aryans to form a central government.

The Medes are known for being fierce warriors and skilled horse breeders. They first inhabited the northern and central areas of the Iranian plateau before setting up their vast empire stretching from present day Afghanistan to Turkey.

____ The Persians penetrated further south and settled in the Elamite province of Parsumash near Anshan.

Here, they inherited the wisdom of the older civilization of the Elamites and enriched this priceless heritage. After the progressive weakening of the Elamite State, the province of Parsumash became the independent homeland of the Persians.

835 The first documented reference to the Persians and the Medes was given by the king of Assyrians, Shalmansar III.

____ Urartians formed an empire stretching from Lake Van in Anatolia to parts of Azerbaijan and northern Mesopotamia.

They excelled in metallurgy and contributed to architecture, the gabled roof being attributed to them. Their capital was Toshya or Toshpa near Lake Van. Urartian architectural remains in Iran are two fortresses, one at Bastam near Maku and one at Sangar.

____ The Medes established the earliest identified fire temple of the Iranian plateau on Teppeh Nushijan.

The 37-meter-high Teppeh Nushijan, 14 km (9 miles) west of Malayer, was occupied by the Medes from about mid-eighth century BC. The well-preserved site with its early Median columned halls and fire temple permits a clear understanding of the plan of this partly-mud-brick complex in which wood was also used.

776 Coroebus of Elis, a cook, won the sprint race in the Olympic Games in Greece.

Although he is the first Olympic champion listed, it is generally accepted that the Games were at the time at least probably 500 years older. Olympic Games were staged at Olympia in honor of Zeus every four years.

728 Median king Diocus unified Median tribes in one super-tribe.

722 The Median city of Hegmataneh, or Ecbatana, was constructed over the ruins of a Kassite settlement.

714 The founder of the Median Empire, Diocus, was deported to Syria by the Assyrians.

710 Elamites led by Shutruk Nahunte II (r.716-699 BC) launched several successful military expeditions into Mesopotamia, each time bringing back considerable riches.

681 Achaemenes was credited with leading the Persians against the Assyrians.

680 Probable date of birth of Prophet Zoroaster.

Prophet Zoroaster, or Zarathustra, founder of Zoroastrian religion, explained that the world was ruled by two principles, Good and Evil, and instructed his followers that by virtue of their adherence to the good, they would help to assure the ultimate triumph of Good over Evil.

640 The Assyrians led by their king, Ashurbanipal (r.668-627 BC), sacked Susa, captured the city of Dur-Untashi, conquered Elam, and ended 23 centuries of Elamite monarchy.

Assyrian idols that were taken five centuries earlier to Elam, were returned to Assyria. By this time both the Medes and Persians had become involved in the shifting alliances that dominated the conflicts between the Elamite, Babylonian and Assyrian Empires.

612 The Medes, under Cyaxares, became so well organized that they eventually managed to bring down the Assyrians.

Appendix 3
Dynasties

Gray entries are not mentioned in the main text.

Achaemenians

Cyrus the Great (Kurosh) .... 559-530 BC
Cambyses II (Kambujiyeh) .... 530-522 BC
Bardia (Smerdis) .... 522-522 BC
Darius the Great (Dariush) .... 522-486 BC
Xerxes I (Khashayarsha) .... 486-465 BC
Artaxerxes I (Ardashir) .... 465-424 BC
Xerxes II (Khashayarsha II) .... 424-423 BC
Darius II (Dariush II) .... 423-404 BC
Artaxerxes II (Ardashir II) .... 404-359 BC
Cyrus the Younger (Kurosh)..................... 401-401 BC
Artaxerxes III (Ardashir III) .... 359-338 BC
Arses .... 338-336 BC
Darius III (Dariush III) .... 336-330 BC

❖ Alexander's occupation

Alexander (Eskandar) .... 334-330 BC

Seleucids

Seleucus (Nicator) .... 312-281 BC
Antiochus (Soter) .... 281-261 BC
Antiochus II (Theos) .... 261-246 BC
Seleucus II (Callinicus)............................ 246-226 BC
Seleucus III (Soter) .... 226-223 BC
Antiochus III (the Great).......................... 223-187 BC
Seleucus IV (Philopator)........................... 187-175 BC
Antiochus IV (Epiphanes) .... 175-163 BC
Antiochus V (Eupator) .... 163-162 BC
Demetrius I (Soter) .... 162-150 BC
Alexander I (Balas) .... 150-145 BC

Antiochus VI (Epiphanes)	145-142 BC
Demitrius II (Nicator)	142-138 BC
Tryphon (Usurper)	142-138 BC
Antiochus VII (Evergetes)	139-129 BC

❖ Parthian domination

Parthians

Arsaces (Arashk)	247-211 BC
Tiridates (Tirdad)	? -211 BC
Artabanus (Arsaces II)	211-191 BC
Priapatius	191-176 BC
Phraates (Farhad)	176-171 BC
Mithradates (Mehrdad)	171-138 BC
Phraates II (Farhad II)	138-128 BC
Artabanus II (Ardavan II)	128-123 BC
Mithradates II (Mehrdad II)	123-87 BC
Gotarzes (Gudarz)	90-80 BC
Orodes (Orod)	80-77 BC
Sinartukes	77-70 BC
Pharaates III (Farhad III)	70-57 BC
Mithradates III (Mehrdad III)	57-54 BC
Orodes II (Orod II)	57-38 BC
Phraates IV (Farhad IV)	38-2 BC
Tiridates II (pretender to the throne)	30-25 BC
Phraates V (Farhad V)	2 BC-4 AD
Orodes III (Orod III)	4-7
Vonones I (Vonon I)	7-12
Artabanus III (Ardavan III)	12-38
Gotarzes II (Gudarz II)	38-51
Vardanes I	39-45
Vonones II (Vonon II)	51-51
Vologeses I	51-78
Vardanes II	55-58
Vologeses II	77-80
Artabanus IV (Ardavan IV)	80-81

Pacores I	78-105
Vologeses III	105-147
Osroes	109-129
Mithradates IV (Mehrdad IV)	129-147
Vologeses IV	147-191
Vologeses V	191-208
Vologeses VI	208-222
Artabanus V (Ardavan V)	213-224

❖ Sassanian conquest

Sassanians

Ardashir	224-240
Shapur	240-272
Hormuz Ardashir	272-273
Bahram	273-276
Bahram II	276-293
Bahram III	293-293
Narseh	293-302
Hormuz II	302-309
Shapur II	309-379
Ardashir II	379-383
Shapur III	383-388
Bahram IV	388-399
Yazdgerd	399-421
Bahram V	421-439
Yazdgerd II	439-457
Hormuz III	457-459
Piruz	459-484
Balash	484-488
Kavad, first reign	488-496
Zamasp	496-498
Kavad, second reign	498-531
Khosrow Anushirvan	531-579
Hormizd IV	579-590
Bahram Chubin	590-591

Khosrow II (Khosrow Parviz) 591-628
Kavad II 628-628
Ardashir III 628-630
Boran (Daughter of Khosrow Parviz) 630-631
Azarmedukht (Sister) 631-632
Khosrow III 630-632
Yazdgerd III 632-651

❖ Muslims conquest

Umayyads Syria

Mu'awiya Ibn Abu Sufyan 661-680
Yazid Ibn Mu'awiya 680-683
Mu'awiya II Ibn Yazid 683-684
Marwan Ibn al-Hakam 684-684
Abdul Malik Ibn Marvan 684-705
Al-Walid Ibn Abdul Malik 705-715
Sulaiman Ibn Abdul Malik 715-717
Umar II Ibn Abdul Aziz Ibn Marwan 717-720
Yazid II Ibn Abdul Malik 720-724
Hisham Ibn Abdul Malik 724-743
Al-Walid II Ibn Yazid II 743-744
Yazid III Ibn al-Walid 744-744
Ibrahim Ibn al-Walid 744-744
Marwan II Ibn Muhammad Ibn al-Hamar . 744-750

Abbasids Iran and Baghdad

As-Saffah 749-754
Al-Mansur 754-775
Al-Mahdi 775-785
Al-Hadi 785-786
Harun ar-Rashid 786-809
Al-Amin 809-813
Al-Ma'mun 813-817
Ibrahim Ibn al-Mahdi 817-819
Al-Mu'tasim 833-842

Al-Wathiq	842-847
Al-Mutawakkil	847-861
Al-Muntasir	861-862
Al-Musta'in	862-866
Al-Mu'tazz	866-869
Al-Muhtadi	869-870
Al-Mu'tamid	870-892
Al-Mu'tadid	892-902
Al-Muktafi	902-908
Al-Mugtadir	908-932
Al-Qahir	932-934
Ar-Radi	934-940
Al-Muttaqi	940-944
Al-Mustakfi	944-946
Al-Muti	946-974
At-Ta'I	974-991
Al-Qadir	991-1031
Al-Qa'im	1031-1075
Al-Muqtadi	1075-1094
Al-Mustazhir	1094-1118
Al-Mustarshid	1118-1135
Ar-Rashid	1135-1136
Al-Muqtafi	1136-1160
Al-Mustanjid	1160-1170
Al-Mustadi	1170-1180
An-Nasir	1180-1225
Az-Zahir	1225-1226
Al-Mustansir	1226-1242
Al-Musta'sim	1242-1258

❖ Mongol sack of Baghdad

Safarids Sistan

Yaqub Leis Saffar	867-879
Amr Ibn Leis	879-901
Tahir Ibn Mohammad	901-908

Leis Ibn Ali	908-910
Mohammad Ibn Ali	910-911
First Samanid Occupation	911-912
Amr Ibn Yaqub	912-913
Second Samanid Occupation	913-922
Ahmad Ibn Mohammad	922-963
Khalaf Ibn Ahmad (Vali od-Dowleh)	963-971

Samanids Khorasan & Transoxiana

Ahmad Ibn Asad Ibn Saman	819-864
Nasr Ibn Ahmad	864-892
Ismail Ibn Ahmad	**892-907**
Ahmad II Ibn Ismail	907-914
Nasr II Ibn Ahmad II	914-943
Nuh Ibn Nasr II	943-954
Abdul Malik Ibn Nuh	954-961
Mansur Ibn Nuh	**961-976**
Nuh II Ibn Mansur	976-997
Mansur II Ibn Nuh II	997-999
Abdol Malik II Ibn Nuh II	999-1000
Ismail II (al-Muntasir)	1000-1005

Tahirids Khorasan

Tahir Ibn Hossein (Zol-Yaninayn)	**821-822**
Talheh	822-828
Abdollah	**828-845**
Tahir II	845-862
Mohammad	862-873

Ziyarids Tabarestan & Gorgan

Mardavij Ibn Ziyar	**927-935**
Voshmgir (Zahir od-Dowleh)	**935-967**
Behsotun (Zahir od-Dowleh)	967-978
Qabus (Shams ol-Ma'ali)	**978-1012**
Manuchehr (Falak ol-Ma'ali)	**1012-1029**

Anushirvan 1029-1049
Key Kavus (Onsur ol-Ma'ali) .... 1049- ?
Gilan Shah .... ? -1090

Buyids Iran & Iraq

Buyids of Fars & Khuzestan

Ali (Emad od-Dowleh) 934-949
Fana Khosrow (Azod od-Dowleh) 949-983
Shirzil (Sharaf od-Dowleh) 983-990
Marzban (Samsaam od-Dowleh) 990-998
Firuz (Baha od-Dowleh) 998-1012
Soltan od-Dowleh 1012-1021
Hasan (Mosharraf od-Dowleh) 1021-1024
Marzban (Emad od-Din) 1024-1048
Khosrow Firuz (Malik or-Rahim) 1048-1055
Fulad Soltan (In Fars only) 1055-1062

❖ Fars occupation by the Kurdish Chief Fazluya

Buyids of Kerman

Ahmad (Mo'ez od-Dowleh) 936-949
Fana Khosrow (Azod od-Dowleh) 949-983
Marzban (Samsaam od-Dowleh) 983-998
Firuz (Baha od-Dowleh) 998-1012
Qavam od-Dowleh 1012-1028
Marzban (Emad od-Din) 1028-1048

❖ Saljuq line of Qawurd

Buyids of Jebal

Ali (Emad od-Dowleh) 932-947
Hasan (Rokn od-Dowleh) 947-977

Buyids of Hamedan and Isfahan

Buya (Mo'ayyed od-Dowleh) 977-983
Ali (Fakhr od-Dowleh) 983-997
Shams od-Dowleh 997-1021

Samad od-Dowleh	1021-1028

<u>Buyids of Reyy</u>

Ali (Fakhr od-Dowleh)	977-997
Rostam (Majd od-Dowleh)	997-1029

❖ Ghaznavid conquest

<u>Buyids of Iraq</u>

Ahmad (Mo'ez od-Dowleh)	945-967
Bakhtiar (Ez od-Dowleh)	967-978
Fana Khosrow (Azod od-Dowleh)	978-983
Marzban (Samsaam od-Dowleh)	983-987
Shirzil (Sharaf od-Dowleh)	987-989
Soltan od-Dowleh	1012-1021
Hassan (Mosharraf od-Dowleh)	1021-1025
Shirzil (Jalal od-Din)	1025-1044
Marzban (Emad od-Din)	1044-1048
Khosrow Firuz (Malik or-Rahim)	1048-1055

❖ Saljuq occupation of Baghdad

<u>Ghaznavids Khorasan, Afghanestan & N. India</u>

Sebuktigin (Nasir od-Dowleh)	971-977
Ismail	977-998
Mahmud (Yamin od-Dowleh)	998-1030
Mohammad (Jalal od-Dowleh), first reign .	1030-1031
Masud (Shihab od-Dowleh)	1031-1041
Mohammad (Jalal od-Dowleh), 2nd reign ..	1041-1041
Mowdud (Shahab od-Dowleh)	1041-1050
Masud II	1050-1050
Ali (Baha od-Dowleh)	1050-1050
Abd or-Rashid (Ez od-Dowleh)	1050-1053
Toghril (Qavam od-Dowleh)	1053-1053
Farrokhzad (Jamal od-Dowleh)	1053-1059
Ebrahim (Zahir od-Dowleh)	1059-1099
Masud III (Ala od-Dowleh)	1099-1115

Shirzad ((Kamal od-Dowleh)	1115-1115
Arsalan Shah (Soltan od-Dowleh)	1115-1118
Bahram Shah (Yamin od-Dowleh)	**1118-1152**
Khosrow Shah (Mo'ez od-Dowleh)	1152-1160
Khosrow Malik (Taj od-Dowleh)	1160-1186

Saljuqs

Toghril (Rokn od-Donya va ad-Din)	**1037-1063**
Alp Arsalan (Azod od-Dowleh)	**1063-1072**
Malik Shah (Jalal od-Dowleh)	**1072-1092**
Mahmud (Nasir od-Din)	1092-1094
Berk Yaruq (Rokn od-Din)	1094-1105
Malik Shah II (Mo'ez od-Din)	1105-1105
Mohammad (Ghias od-Din)	1105-1118
Sanjar (Mo'ez od-Din)	**1118-1157**

Saljuqs of Western Persia

Mahmud II (Moghis od-Din)	1118-1131
Davud (Ghias od-Din)	1131-1132
Toghril II (Rokn od-Din)	1132-1134
Masud (Ghias od-Din)	1134-1153
Mohammad II (Rokn od-Din)	1153-1160
Solayman Shah (Ghias od-Din)	1160-1161
Arsalan (Mo'ez od-Din)	1161-1176
Toghril III (Rokn od-Din)	**1176-1194**

❖ Khawrazm-Shahs domination

Saljuqs of Kerman

Qavurd (Imad od-Din)	**1041-1073**
Kermanshah	1073-1074
Hossein	1074-1074
Soltanshah (Rokn od-Dawla)	1074-1085
Turanshah (Mohy od-Din)	1085-1097
Iranshah (Baha od-Din)	1097-1101
Arsalan Shah (Mohy od-Din)	1101-1142

Mohammad (Moghith od-Din)	1142-1156
Toghril Shah (Mohy od-Din)	1156-1170
Bahram Shah	1170-1175
Arsalan Shah II	1175-1176
Mohammad II	1183-1186

❖ Oghuz occupation

Khwarazm-Shahs

Anushtegin	1077-1098
Qutb od-Din Mohammad	1098-1128
Ala'eddin Atsiz Ibn Qotb od-Din	1128-1156
Il-Arsalan	1156-1172
Mohammad Sultanshah Ibn Ilarsalan	1172-1193
Tekish Ibn Ilarsalan (Ala od-Din)	1172-1200
Ala od-Din Mohammad	1200-1220
Jalal od-Din	1220-1231

Atabegs of Fars

Sonqor	1148-1162
Zangi	1162-1175
Takla	1175-1195
Sa'd	1195-1226
Abu Bakr	1226-1260
Mohammad	1260-1262
Mohammad Shah	1262-1262
Saljuq Shah	1262-1263
Abish	1263-1287

Mongols

Hulagu	1256-1265
Abaqa	1256-1282
Ahmad Tiguder	1282-1284
Arghun	1284-1291
Gaykhatu	1291-1295
Baydu	? -1295

Mahmud Ghazan	1295-1304
Oljeitu (Mohammad Khodabanda)	1304-1316
Abu Sa'id	1316-1335
Arpa	1335-1336
Musa	1336-1353

Muzaffirids Southern Iran

Mohammad Ibn Muzafar(Mobariz od-Din)	1314-1358
Shah Mahmud (Qotb od-Din)	1358-1364
Shah Shoja (Jalal od-Din)	1364-1384
Zayn ol-Abidin Ali (Mojahid od-Din)	1384-1387
Yahya (Nosrat od-Din) of Yazd	1387-1393
Mansur of Isfahan, Fars & Iraq	1387-1393

Jalalirids Azarbayjan, Kurdestan & Iraq

Hassan Bozorg (Taj od-Din)	1336-1356
Oways	1356-1374
Hossein (Jalal od-Din)	1374-1382
Ahmad (Ghias od-Din)	1382-1410
Bayazid of Kurdestan	1382-1383
Shah Walad	1410-1411
Mahmud, first reign	1411-1415
Oways II	1415-1421
Mohammad	1421-1422
Mahmud, second reign	1422-1424
Hossein II	1424-1432

Timurids Transoxania & Iran

Timurids of Samarqand

Timur (Timurlane)	1370-1405
Khalil	1370-1409
Shahrokh	1405-1447
Ulugh Beg	1447-1449
Abdul Latif	1449-1450
Abdollah Mirza	1450-1451

Abu Sa'id 1451-1469
Ahmad 1469-1494
Mahmud Ibn Abu Sa'id 1494-1500

Timurids of western Iran after Timur

Miranshah **1404-1409**
Khalil 1409-1414
Ayyal 1414-1414
Aylankar 1414-1415

Timurids of Khorasan after Ulugh Beg

Babur 1449-1457
Mahmud Ibn Babur 1457-1459
Abu Sa'id 1459-1469
Yadegar Mohammad 1469-1470
Hossein Baqara 1470-1506
Badi oz-Zaman 1506-

Qara Quyunlu Azarbaijan & Iraq

Qara Mohammad Turmush 1380-1389
Qara Yusof 1389-1400

❖ Timurid invasion

Qara Yusof, reinstated 1406-1420
Iskandar 1420-1438
Jahan Shah **1438-1467**
Hassan Ali 1467-1468

Aq Quyunlu Diyarbakir, E. Anatolia & Azarbayjan

Qara Othman (Yuluk) 1378-1435
Hamza 1435-1438
Jahangir 1444-1453
Uzaun Hassan 1453-1478
Khalil 1478-1490
Ya'qub 1478-1490
Baysonqor 1490-1493

Rostam	1493-1497
Ahmad Govde	1497-1497
Morad of Qom	1497-1498
Alvand of of Azarbayjan	1498-1504
Mohammad Mirza of Fars	1498-1500
Morad	1502-1508

Safavids

Isma'il I	1502-1524
Tahmasp I	1524-1576
Isma'il II	1576-1578
Mohammad Khoda-Banda	1578-1587
Abbas I	1588-1629
Safi I	1629-1642
Abbas II	1642-1667
Soleiman (Safi II)	1667-1694
Sultan Hossein	1694-1722
Tahmasb II	1722-1732

Afsharids

Nadir Shah	1736-1747
Adel Shah	1747-1748
Ebrahim	1748-1748
Shahrokh of Khorasan	1748-1796
Nadir Mirza of Khorasan	1797-1802

Zands

Mohammad Karim Khan	1750-1779
Abol Fath & Mohammad Ali	1779-1779
Sadiq of Shiraz	1779-1781
Ali Morad of Isfahan	1779-1785
Jafar	1785-1785
Lotf Ali Khan	1789-1794

Qajars

Aqa Mohammad Khan	1779-1797

Fath Ali Shah	1797-1834
Mohammad Shah	1834-1848
Nasereddin Shah	1848-1896
Mozafareddin Shah	1896-1907
Mohammad Ali Shah	1907-1909
Ahamd Shah	1909-1924

Pahlavis

Reza Shah	1925-1941
Mohammad Reza Shah	1941-1979

❖ Islamic Revolution

Appendix 4
Early Islamic Leaders

Prophet Mohammad (S)

Prophet Mohammad (S) (al-Mostafa) 570-632

Rashidin ("Orthodox") Caliphs

Abu Bakr as-Siddiq 632-634
Umar Ibn al-Khattab 634-644
Uthman Ibn Affan 644-656
Ali Ibn Abutalib (A) 656-661

Shia Imams

1 Ali Ibn Abi Talib (A) (al-Morteza) 597-661
2 Hassan Ibn Ali (A) (al-Mojtaba) 625-680
3 Hossein Ibn Ali (A) (Aba-Abdullah) 626-680
4 Ali Ibn al-Hossain (A) (Zein ol-Abedin) 657-715
5 Mohammad Ibn Ali (A) (al-Baqir) 676-733
6 Jafar Ibn Mohammad (A) (al-Sadiq) 703-765
7 Musa Ibn Jafar (A) (al-Kazim) 747-800
8 Ali Ibn Musa (A) (ar-Reza) 765-818
9 Mohammad Ibn Ali (A) (at-Taqi) 812-836
10 Ali Ibn Mohammad (A) (an-Naqi) 828-869
11 Hassan Ibn Ali (A) (al-Asgari) 839-875
12 Mohammad Ibn Hassan (A) (al-Mahdi) ..... 870- ...

A

I

J

K

L

M

N

Q

R

S

T